Obstruction of Justice

The Nuns of Sovu in Belgium

February 2000

A Publication of African Rights

11 Marshalsea Road   **Tel: 0171 7717 1224**
London SE1 1EP   **Fax: 0171 717 1240**

Contents

Préfectures in Rwanda

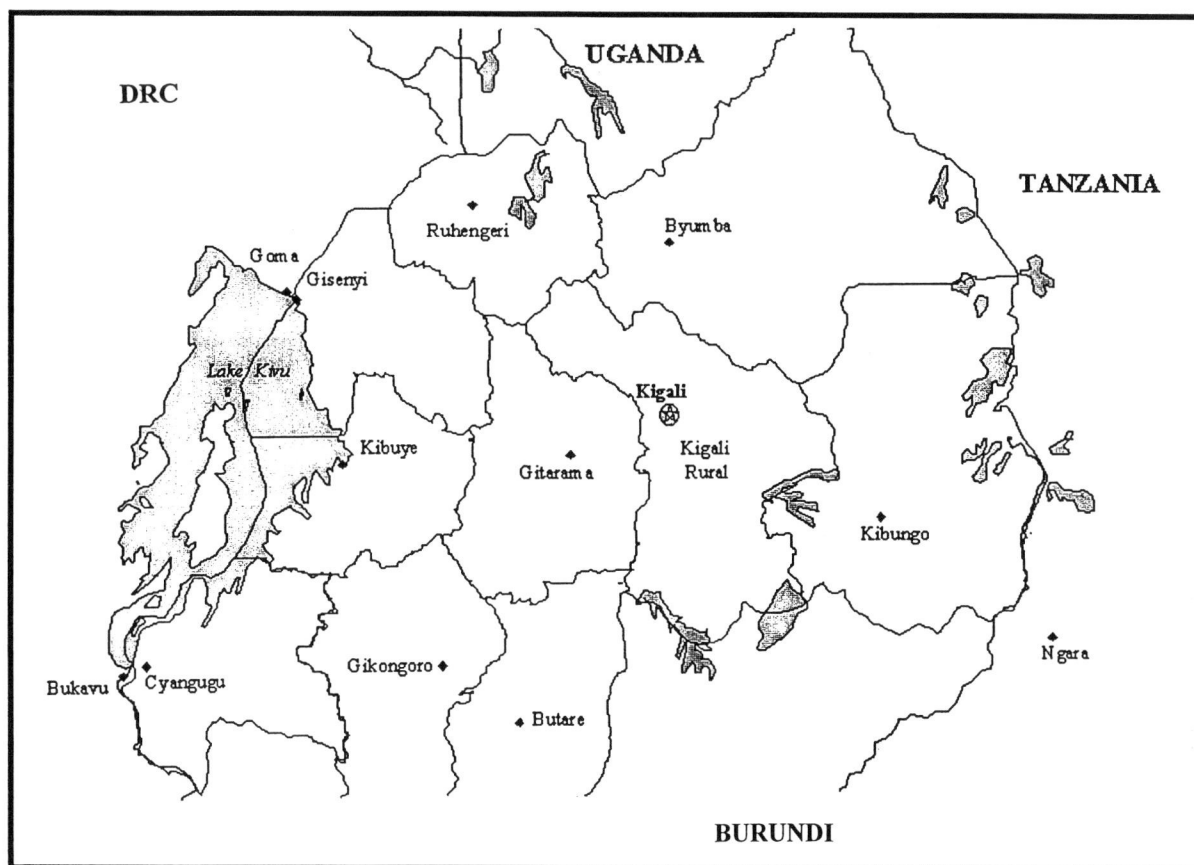

Butare Préfecture in Rwanda

Introduction

This is not the first time that African Rights has published a report about Sr. Gertrude Mukangango and Sr. Julienne Kizito. Four years ago, details of the nuns' behaviour during the genocide in Sovu were included in a book about women's participation in the genocide: *Rwanda: Not So Innocent; When Women Become Killers.* The nuns have since been the subject of a number of television documentaries and several newspaper articles. Yet today they both remain in Belgium, and they continue to receive protection from the Benedictine order, to which they belong. We have pursued our investigation into the accusations against the nuns, and this report brings forward many new witnesses and the highly incriminating testimony of the leader of the interahamwe militia in Sovu, Warrant Officer Emmanuel Rekeraho. He admits his own central role in the massacres at the monastery during the genocide, but he also confirms the many strong and consistent accounts of the direct part played by the two nuns in facilitating and encouraging the militia.

The report builds an account of the events in Sovu between April-July 1994 from the testimonies of 34 witnesses—survivors, fellow-nuns, prisoners accused of genocide and residents of Sovu. From the first moment the refugees arrived in Sovu they were confronted by the negative attitude of Sr. Gertrude, the Mother Superior, who made it clear that she had no intention of giving them shelter. In desperation the refugees tried every means to enter the monastery, but they were soon forced out on the orders of Sr. Gertrude by the communal policemen who were guarding the building. The majority of them then gathered in the area around the health centre which was attached to the monastery. They stood in the pouring rain for days, while the monastery building itself was empty. They were deprived of food and medical care. They became an obvious target for the soldiers and militia.

Under the supervision of Emmanuel Rekeraho, the militia prepared for a massacre which was to wipe out thousands. The nuns collaborated with Rekeraho; they met with him on numerous occasions and they even lent him a minibus. On 22 April, Tutsi men, women and children were stoned, hacked and burned to death at the health centre. Sr. Kizito handed out petrol to the killers, enabling them to burn down a garage in which a group of the refugees were hiding. So comprehensive was the slaughter that we have been unable to locate a single male survivor in Sovu since we began our investigation in 1995.

In the following months, as the militia attempted to finish off any survivors at Sovu, Sr. Gertrude made it clear that she was as determined as they to rid the monastery of any remaining Tutsis. She even expected the Tutsi nuns to hand over their own relatives to the militia, and when they refused to do so, she called for the militia and exposed them herself.

Most of the nuns left Rwanda at the beginning of July, after the military defeat of the interim regime. They were taken in by the Benedictine order in Belgium. They had a special relationship with the nuns as the monastery of Sovu was founded in 1959 by Belgian nuns from Maredret. Gertrude had been at the monastery since 1979 and was appointed Mother Superior on 2 July 1993. Kizito entered the monastery in 1986. But in Belgium the divisions within the Sovu community soon became apparent. Most of the Sisters were very distressed about the conduct of the Mother Superior and Sr. Kizito during the genocide. Some had witnessed the murders of members of their own families and they spoke out about the circumstances of their death. While in Rwanda they had been powerless to challenge the authority of Sr. Gertrude, but in Belgium they were to find that her hold over the community had strengthened. The Mother Superior was given wholehearted support by the Catholic Church authorities in Belgium. Her version of the events in Sovu was accepted and repeated by the head of the Benedictine order and by other members of the clergy. She and Sr. Kizito were considered the "victims" and the nuns who tried to tell their stories were deemed "liars." Sr. Gertrude was herself given the opportunity to publicly respond to the allegations and she calmly denied them, describing her accusers as "traumatised."

The Benedictines have shown unquestioning faith in a senior member of their order, but this fact alone cannot explain why Sr. Gertrude and Sr. Kizito remain at liberty when there are so many people prepared to testify to their involvement in the genocide in Sovu. The example of the Church's response to the accusations against the Sovu nuns raises, once again, the broader issue of the Catholic Church's political stance before, during and after the 1994 genocide. This is a very sensitive issue and one which the Church has failed to tackle with any sincerity. Thousands of churchpeople were among the victims of the genocide, and there were also many who risked their own lives to save terrified refugees. But the list of the bishops, priests and nuns who have been implicated in the killings is also long, and only a handful of them have been arrested or brought to justice.[1] Within the Catholic Church itself there are many individuals who are critical of the Church's response to accusations against the clergy, but their voices have been silenced or ignored.[2] It is not too late for the Church to demonstrate its willingness to support the process of justice in Rwanda.

The idea that nuns can have taken part in genocide challenges all our preconceived notions about evil and its perpetrators. If justice is to be done, we must be able to set these aside and examine the evidence against Sr. Gertrude and Sr. Kizito without prejudice. Our own sense of shock and disbelief at the crimes of which these nuns are accused cannot be compared with that experienced by all the witnesses and survivors whose testimonies are in this report. They fled to the monastery at Sovu believing they would find protection there; instead they were betrayed by the Mother Superior and Sr. Kizito. Their decision to speak out about what happened to them there has itself been a source of suffering as they relive the most painful moments of their lives. If the Catholic Church should again fail to listen to their stories and act upon them, it will be a further rejection and one more wound that they will have to bear.

---

[1] See African Rights' *Open Letter to Pope John Paul II*, 14 May 1998 and African Rights' *Father Wenceslas Munyeshyaka: In the Eyes of the Survivors of Ste. Famille*, Witness to Genocide, Issue 9, April 1999.
[2] See *Memorandum to His Holiness John Paul 11*, March 1996, written by a group of survivors in Kigali.

When Charity Does Not Begin at Home

"Sister Gertrude demonstrated that she was without pity towards the refugees."

When people first realised their lives were at risk in April 1994, often their first thought was that they would find safety in a church and support from the clergy. This was the case in Sovu, as it was all over Rwanda. But when they reached the Benedictine monastery, the refugees faced a situation they could never have imagined. They were denied entry by the very person they expected would protect them. The Mother Superior of the Benedictine nuns, Sister Gertrude Mukangango, showed greater concern for the church buildings than for the men, women and children who tried every means to persuade her to give them shelter. Soon the gates of the monastery were shut as they had never been before, but even so, thousands managed to gain an entry into the church compound. The refugees were left to stand outside the health centre attached to the monastery in the heavy rains. The nuns were forbidden to allow anyone inside either the church or the many empty rooms of the monastery. They were also prevented from giving them food and there was no effort to treat the many wounded who had fled there following attacks by the militia on their homes. As a voice of authority in the monastery as well as in the wider community, Sr. Gertrude's behaviour set an example of the utmost cruelty. She spoke of the refugees as an irritation, "rubbish" which was soiling the church and should be "disposed of." She demonstrated clearly her own ethnic prejudice, and found an ally in Sister Kizito who assisted her in her many attempts to remove the Tutsis from the monastery.

For the first week after Habyarimana's death, the sector of Sovu in commune Huye, Butare, remained calm. Butare, in the south of Rwanda, had been the préfecture least affected by ethnic violence in the past and its residents were thought of as politically liberal. Indeed it was the only region which in 1994 had a Tutsi préfet, Jean-Baptiste Habyarimana. But the people of Sovu were aware of the violence erupting in other areas. There was the constant threat that it would spread from the neighbouring commune of Maraba where militiamen had begun killing Tutsis soon after Habyarimana's assassination. In an effort to ensure the security of the residents of Sovu, Hutu and Tutsi men formed joint patrols. The Tutsi men decided to send women, children and the elderly to the health centre which was attached to the Benedictine monastery in cellule Kigarama, while they remained on the hilltops to ward off attacks by the militia. But as the violence increased the unity of the local people was destroyed and the Tutsi men fled to join their families.

The refugees believed that, as one survivor said, "it was forbidden to kill people who were in God's house." Massacres in churches were unheard of in the killings directed at Tutsis before 1994.[3] Tutsis from Sovu also fled to the Catholic Parish of Rugango and the Benedictine monastery of Gihindamuyaga. But those who sought sanctuary at the Benedictine monastery of Sovu found that they were not welcome. Sr. Gertrude repeatedly made it clear that she resented their presence and refused them entry to the church buildings, but she was unable to get them to leave the health centre. As the intentions of the Sovu militiamen became apparent, Tutsis at the health centre felt extremely vulnerable; it did not have sufficient shelter for the thousands of people who had gathered there and the refugees were cold and hungry. They again turned to the Benedictine nuns for comfort and practical assistance.

Most of the nuns felt pity at the plight of the refugees. They knew there was plenty of space inside the monastery where they could have hidden, but because of the response of the Mother Superior, they were powerless to assist them. Régine Niyonsaba, 31, is from Kigarama. She was a novice in 1994 and is now a student in Save, Butare. She told of what happened when the refugees first arrived.

> The monastery church was open, so they went inside. As soon as the Mother Superior saw them enter the church, she ran over and told them to get out and go home. They did leave, but they came back to

---

[3] In particular there were killings directed at Tutsis in 1959 and 1961-63.

the monastery at about 4:00 p.m. This time they headed for the health centre, where they stayed. There were many of them, and more and more kept coming. Gertrude kept telling them to leave the monastery, but they were reluctant to go.

Eugénie Mukagatera, 28, a native of Karambo in Gikongoro, was also a novice at the monastery.

Many Tutsis from Sovu and neighbouring sectors took refuge at Sovu health centre since the Mother Superior had refused them refuge in the monastery. She said that she didn't want her monastery to be destroyed on account of Tutsis.

It was the rainy season and there were torrential downpours.

One day it rained heavily. These refugees, who were very many, could not all take shelter at the health centre and wanted to come inside the compound of the monastery. They reached the entrance, but the gate was locked tightly. The small children behind the gate were crying a lot, trembling and grinding their teeth because of the rain. All the nuns, except the Mother Superior, Gertrude Mukangango, wanted to shelter these unhappy people. Sister Kizito was not in the monastery. She spent all her time circulating outside.

"Sr. Mathilde Ndererimana said to Gertrude: 'How can you pretend to welcome Jesus who knocks at the door without welcoming those people who are knocking at the door behind the gate? The Jesus we speak about is well and truly represented in them?' Gertrude did not react."

Sisters like Fortunata, Bernadette and Marie-Bernard also insisted that these people be welcomed. The refugees continued to suffer without nourishment, without any assistance on the part of the monastery.

Mélanie, a pseudonym for a nun who requested anonymity, spoke of their helplessness in the face of the refugees' needs and Gertrude's stubbornness.

It was in the afternoon that the refugees took shelter in our monastery. It rained heavily. The refugees wanted to come inside the monastery buildings, but Gertrude Mukangango refused. She locked all the doors to the houses so that the refugees had nowhere to shelter.

Faced with the cries of the children, the wailing and the shaking of the soaked refugees, nearly all the Sisters told Gertrude that she should let the refugees take shelter. There was no shortage of space; the monastery had the use of a hostelry, a chapel and other empty rooms. But Gertrude refused. She told us that we wanted all the responsibility to be placed on her shoulders. It rained for several hours and it was horrible to see how the innocent people hardly moved under such torrential rain. It continued raining until 7:00 p.m.

There were some communal policemen who were pretending to guard the monastery. That same evening, Sr. Gertrude asked them to force the refugees to go back to the health centre. The policemen did so very quickly.

Gertrude demonstrated that she was without pity towards the refugees. She did not even hesitate to hand them over, chasing them from the monastery under very difficult circumstances. Gertrude showed herself to be without pity for the Tutsi refugees, in all the suffering they endured during the genocide in Sovu.

For the refugees themselves, the situation was bleak and their choices were limited. 35-year-old Caritas[4] is the younger sister of one of the nuns at the monastery. On 17 April, Caritas decided to visit her parents in her commune of origin, also in Butare. Her husband accompanied her. Within minutes of their arrival, her parents' home was attacked with gunfire and grenades. Finding other roads blocked, they headed for Sovu to join her sister at the monastery. They arrived at about 1:30

---

[4] Caritas is a pseudonym.

p.m. and found her father already there. Caritas' husband then left as he was Hutu and his life was not at risk.

> We had just entered the courtyard of the monastery when a grenade exploded below us, down in Sovu forest. This caused panic among the refugees who were staying close to the health centre. They ran to get inside the walls of the monastery, filling the courtyards and porches of various houses. It was the rainy season and people needed shelter.
> The next day, Sr. Gertrude threatened us in an attempt to make us leave the monastery. We refused to move, asking her where on earth she expected us to go.[5]

Caritas and her father were hidden inside the monastery by her sister.

Like the other refugees, Marie-Goretti Mbateye, 42, had no choice but to sneak into the monastery through the hedges and barbed wire. Marie-Goretti, a farmer at the time, is now a trader and secretary to the councillor of Sovu.

> We helped the others who were climbing in so that they would not hurt themselves or fall and break a limb. During this time, Gertrude and Kizito were on the landing, watching and mocking us instead of opening the doors for us. They were laughing. Their laughter really shocked us. We approached Kizito. She chased us away, saying that we were disturbing the people attending a meeting and that we should go down to the health centre. She said she couldn't see what we were fleeing from. We stayed at the monastery until the evening. During the night, it poured with rain. My mother, my sisters and their children and I tried to take cover under my umbrella. That night, Sr. Scholastique came and asked Mpambara to tell Gertrude to open two rooms for us so that those with children could shelter there. But Sr. Gertrude only made one room available. This room was too small and too hot. Because of the heat, we took turns staying inside. Others, especially the men, slid underneath the vehicles. I sat on a mat on the grass in this rain. I left the umbrella for my mother. It rained the whole night, until about 3:00 a.m. You would have thought that even the heavens didn't want us anymore.[6]

Renata Gatesi, then aged 16, was one of the youngsters who was allowed inside the monastery for a short time. Renata's family were farmers in Kigarama, and her uncle, Augustin Mpambara, was a worker at the monastery. They went to the monastery on the 19th , she said, "because we could see that it was too dangerous at the health centre, even though we'd been advised by Sr. Gertrude and Sr. Kizito to stay there."

> The monastery gate was shut. We tried to climb in, even pregnant women were climbing. Others managed to get in through the cypress hedge and in-between the barbed wire. Chantal Kayigirwa was trying to climb in when she fell off together with her baby, injuring her head. Meanwhile, Gertrude and Kizito were upstairs, watching the distressing spectacle. Kizito came down and complained about the noise we were making. She told us to go and occupy the volley-ball field. The relatives of the Tutsi nuns, and relatives of the employees of the monastery were inside. Kizito came and took the children, myself included, into the cellar where they made communion wafers, but she came back later and drove us out. She kept all of our possessions. That evening it poured with rain. The nuns gave us no food or shelter. It was Sr. Scholastique who came and asked my uncle, Mpambara, to open up a room for the women and babies. We had been using mattresses to keep out the rain, but they were already soaked. The room Mpambara opened was too small for everyone to get in, and too hot inside. Some people preferred the rain to that heat. Others, especially the young, chose to lie underneath the cars of people attending a conference at the monastery. There were two communal policemen on guard, Xavier Nsanzabera and Joseph Bizimana. Some others I didn't know had also come to keep watch at the monastery. [7]

Alphonsine Mukamudenge, 47, a farmer from Karuhaya cellule in Sovu, reached the monastery on the 17th. She explained why her family decided to flee there.

---

[5] Interviewed in Butare, 29 November 1995.
[6] Interviewed in Sovu, 14 July 1999.
[7] Interviewed in Sovu, 14 July 1999.

Since the area belonged to monks and nuns, we felt protected against the assassins. Unfortunately, the opposite was true. The same night we arrived, Gertrude and Kizito got angry. Gertrude said: "The Tutsis are insane. They say that they have fled because the Hutus are threatening them. Yet now, they are saying these words in front of other Hutus." On the morning of 18 April, Gertrude said: "I don't want all this rubbish here; we must dispose of them somewhere because this is giving me a headache."[8]

Juliette Mukangango left her home in Kigarama on the 17th, accompanied by her children—Augustin, 14, Géraldine, ten and Viateur, seven. Her husband had died in 1989. They went straight to the monastery.

When we arrived at the monastery, the gates were shut, contrary to the usual practice. The ones who could climb in did so, but the women couldn't manage. The people who were already inside made a hole in the wall, and we had to crawl through it to get in. Sr. Scholastique came out and asked the workman, Mpambara, to provide shelter for the sick, the mothers and children. He opened up and everyone wanted to get in, but there was not enough room for everyone; so some stayed outside. The communal policeman, Joseph Bizimana, was there. He wanted us to all squeeze inside so that he could keep an eye on us all and stop anyone from escaping.

Sr. Gertrude Mukangango came that morning to drive us out of the courtyard. She said that we were making the monastery dirty, and that if we refused to leave she would call soldiers. She begged us to leave. We refused. Again she threatened to bring in the soldiers.[9]

Vestine[10] from Sovu sector, joined the refugees on the 17th.

I fled to the Benedictine Sisters in Sovu because I knew that no-one could kill someone who was in a church or who had come into a monastery. I had the opposite experience because even the Sisters refused to give us a place to hide. Sr. Kizito said to me: "I don't want the *Inyenzi* hiding here. You don't like peace, so you must suffer the consequences." On the morning of 18 April, Kizito and Sr. Gertrude made us come out of the church so that we would not soil the church, nor the front of the church.[11]

Lambert Nsabimana's Tutsi wife, Françoise Nyandwi, abandoned her house for the health centre on the 17th. Lambert, 36, a farmer from Kigarama, is Hutu and remained at home. On the 18th, he learned that a grenade had been lobbed at the health centre; he decided to transfer Françoise to the monastery.

The main gate was shut which was unusual for the monastery. But the refugees inside helped us to make a hole in the wall, and we got in. It rained in the evening. Sr. Scholastique took pity on the mothers and children, and asked Mpambara to open some rooms for the women and children. The men stayed outside because the cellar was hot and cramped.[12]

Chantal Mukamisha, 27, a farmer from Karuhaya, said a few of the refugees did manage to get inside the monastery buildings, but she was not among them.

On Sunday the 17th, as we felt under threat, we left our homes and went into hiding with the nuns in the monastery and the health centre. The Mother Superior didn't want to let us in, but we had no choice. Some of us stayed in the health centre, while others went back to the monastery. Some got into their rooms, including my mother, Aimée-Marie Mujawamariya, my sister and her children.

---

[8] Interviewed in Sovu, 9 May 1996.

[9] Interviewed in Sovu, 28 May 1999.

[10] This is a pseudonym.

[11] Interviewed in Sovu, 9 May 1996.

[12] Interviewed in Sovu, 28 May 1999.

We were in the courtyard. It rained that evening and we were outside with nowhere to shelter from it. Some people sheltered under the vehicles belonging to the nuns.[13]

Forced Out at Gunpoint

On 19 April the President of the interim government, Dr. Théodore Sindikubwabo, a native of Butare, met with local officials in Butare in Butare. He publicly criticised the people of Butare for acting as if they were "unconcerned" (*Ntibindeba)* about the killing of Tutsis elsewhere in the country. His visit signalled the official launch of the genocide throughout the préfecture of Butare. Neighbouring communes were by now fully committed to the policy of massacres. The Tutsi men and boys who had taken part in joint patrols realised that they could not hold out against the troops of the genocide, who were now united and who had received official backing. They too were now in search of a place to hide. Terrified by the sound of gunfire and grenades, Tutsis tried to force their way into the monastery, either by making gaps in the cypress trees or by jumping over the wall.

As the refugees became more desperate and determined to stay in the monastery, Sr. Gertrude ignored their pleas and called for soldiers to remove them forcibly. Consolée Mukeshimana, 34, comes from Ruhashya in Butare and had worked at the health centre run by the Benedictine Sisters for eight years. When she was advised to flee by a Hutu neighbour, she went directly to the monastery as she knew the nuns well. She found the entry gate locked, but squeezed through a gap that the other refugees made in the wall. She then hid in a room with three other refugees but was soon discovered by the Mother Superior.

> Gertrude Mukangango threatened us [telling us] to leave the room and get outside. We refused and told her that we were going to die down there. She told me that I would regret it. Immediately she went out and took the new car, a Mazda minibus that had just been bought, and she left. Some minutes later, she came back with a communal policeman, Joseph Bizimana, and six soldiers in her minibus. She came where we were. She told the soldiers, and I quote: "There they are. They refused to leave our room." With guns and kicks, the soldiers quickly pushed us outside. At the time, I was pregnant.

The refugees assumed that it would be sufficient to vacate the interior buildings and to assemble in the courtyard. But Gertrude did not want the refugees anywhere near the monastery.

> We arrived outside. There were a lot of refugees sitting in the courtyard of the chapel of Sovu. Gertrude told the soldiers to make us leave the monastery, saying that the monastery must not be destroyed on account of Tutsis. The soldiers [wanted to make] us all return to the health centre. We refused but we could not hold out in the face of such a threat.[14]

Some of the refugees interpreted the arrival of Gertrude and the gendarmes as a sign of hope. Renata Gatesi, then a teenager, was one of them.

> We were overjoyed, thinking that they had come to help the communal policemen to protect us. They gathered us together outside the church. Gertrude spoke to a gendarme; then they went down to the health centre and back again. They told us to go to the centre where no-one would come and bother us. They said: "We can either guard you there, or you'll have to go back home." The gendarme added: "You're not refugees. The real refugees are the ones from Nyacyonga [15] who have fled the RPF. You people have light, water, and mattresses; so how can you call yourselves refugees? And who are you running away from anyway?"
>
> We said that we were afraid the militiamen would come and kill us, but they insisted. Gertrude and two gendarmes went to the gate to stop us getting back into the monastery. We all went down to

---

[13] Interviewed in Sovu, 28 May 1999.

[14] Interviewed in Ngoma, 21 July 1995.

[15] Nyacyonga, on the outskirts of Kigali, was a camp for the Hutu residents of the Byumba region displaced since 1990 by the war between the RPF and the FAR.

the health centre, apart from the relatives of the nuns and of the employees of the monastery. But later the employees' relatives came down and joined us.

Ruth Mugorewase, 22, has lived in Sovu all her life. She was employed by the Benedictine Sisters in Sovu at the time of the interview. Ruth and her family, who lived close by, arrived at the monastery on the 17th. They felt sure they would be protected there, but they soon realised that the militia held nothing sacred.

The following day, there were many people in front of the church and the monastery, armed with machetes, *massues* and swords; some of them even had rifles and grenades. Gertrude Mukangango calmed them down so that she could go and get the bourgmestre of Huye, Jonathan Ruremesha. They came together with two soldiers. The bourgmestre asked the population who had all these arms: "Who amongst you knows how to lob a grenade?" Of course we were shocked and shaking.[16]

Ruth discovered that the Mother Superior and Sr. Kizito were concerned only about the fate of the few Hutus who were in the monastery.

Gertrude told the bourgmestre: "It seems that there are some Hutu women. We must make them come out from this crowd of nasty people." Gertrude even went to the rooms in the church to tell the people who were there to come out immediately. Gertrude told the bourgmestre: "I don't want this rubbish in front of the church; it is necessary to look for another place to dispose of them." Meanwhile, Sr. Kizito was asking: "If there are any Hutus, they should stand to one side?" I will never, in my life, forget the participation of Gertrude Mukangango and Julienne Kizito in the genocide of the Tutsi people in Sovu.

Alphonsine Mukamudenge said the bourgmestre, Jonathan Ruremesha, incited the Hutus to violence.

Gertrude asked the people near the church, armed with machetes, swords and *massues*, to be quiet. She calmed them down, then she went to see Ruremesha in Huye commune to find out how they should behave, faced with this situation. They came back with two well-armed policemen. The bourgmestre asked the Hutus who were there this question: "Are you ready to kill the Tutsis?". That was the slogan.

Séraphine Mukamana was one of those who had managed to get inside the monastery.

The Mother Superior, Gertrude Mukangango, came to make us get out. But we refused. She left in her Mazda car. After a few minutes, she came back, this time with a communal policeman, the head of the communal police force of Huye, Joseph Bizimana, and six soldiers. Gertrude led them to the room where we were hiding. These soldiers forced us out and we quickly went down the stairs. When we got to the courtyard of the monastery, these same soldiers forced all the refugees to take their bags and go down to the health centre. Gertrude said that we constituted some sort of dirt in the monastery and that we were even disturbing the visitors who were there on a training course.

Adelice Mukabutera is Séraphine's younger sister.

The Mother Superior, Gertrude, didn't want us to stay. She said that we were dirt in the monastery and that we were disturbing the visitors who were there for training. She called the soldiers from Butare [town] who came and forced us to leave the monastery and go, once again, to the health centre.

Josée Mukarwego, the mother of seven children, had been at the monastery since the 17th.

The Mother Superior, Gertrude, and Sr. Kizito came. They told us that we constituted dirt in the monastery, on account of which we should leave a place that was sacred. We refused. Gertrude took her car and she brought soldiers. It was about 2:00 p.m. When they came, the soldiers forced us to go back to the health centre.

---

[16] Interviewed in Sovu, 9 May 1996.

The monastery of Sovu

Domatile Mukabanza was carrying her youngest when she approached the gate of the monastery. Realising it was locked, she crawled through the barbed wire with the baby strapped to her back.

> There were a lot of us down there. Many of the refugees gathered around the chapel which was also locked tightly. It was then that Sr. Gertrude Mukangango came out in order to threaten us into leaving the monastery. She was accompanied by Sr. Julienne Kizito, originally from Sovu. We refused and Gertrude took the Mazda minibus. She came back with six soldiers who were well armed and the head of the communal police force. She asked these soldiers to make us come out of the monastery. She told them that she did not want the blood of Tutsis in the monastery. Small children begged her to hide them. But she shoved them off outside, telling them to follow their parents. These soldiers told us to sit down in front of the chapel. Afterwards, they forced us to go back to the health centre where we spent the night.[17]

Marie-Goretti Mbateye, soaked by the heavy rainfall of the night before, was warming herself in the sun when Sr. Gertrude and the gendarmes called the refugees together in front of the church to explain that they must leave the monastery. Marie-Goretti spoke of their sense of disbelief.

> In a loud voice, Gertrude told us that we just had to go to the health centre as this was the place she had allocated to us. The gendarme who had gone down to the health centre with her asked us: "What are you fleeing from? The true refugees are those at Nyacyonga." We went down to the health centre; we didn't have a choice. There were children crying from hunger and from lack of sleep, pregnant women and elderly people who, because they had not committed any wrong, didn't understand anything. We were alone, looking death in the face, abandoned even by women who claimed to have given themselves to God. Why chase us away from the monastery? At least if they had not worn the veil.

Because he was able to walk around, Lambert Nsabimana was aware of the peril that awaited the refugees.

> On Tuesday 19 April, Gertrude and Kizito called us together outside their chapel to persuade us to leave the monastery. In view of the situation, they must have known very well what would happen to the Tutsis. Besides, Kizito comes from this area. She had relatives among the militia and used to chat to them.

Juliette Mukangango said that soldiers threatened the refugees and later that night they attacked them.

> One of them called Sr. Gertrude aside and spoke to her. They told us to get our belongings and go down to the health centre. This soldier said to us, "Do you think you've escaped? Who ever fled, taking their mattress and motorbike with them?" That night they threw a hand grenade in which wounded an old woman, Pascasie Nyiramirimo. The policemen fired into the air and we panicked.

Meetings With the Militia

Warrant Officer Emmanuel Rekeraho, the commander of the local interahamwe, was a regular visitor to the monastery. From April-July 1994, Rekeraho was the most feared man in Sovu, responsible for planning and implementing massacres of thousands of people. It was he who organised the massacres at the health centre and the monastery. His good relations with Sr. Gertrude and Sr. Kizito have been commented upon by the other nuns and by survivors. Their willingness to meet and collaborate with Rekeraho links them closely to the atrocities.

Rekeraho, 61, comes from Rusagara in the neighbouring commune of Maraba in Butare. He left the army in 1977, and was employed in a fertiliser programme in commune Runyinya, Butare, when

---

[17] Interviewed in Sovu, 21 July 1995.

the genocide began.[18] He said that he became acquainted with Gertrude and Kizito before 1994, but that "it was especially during the genocide that he got to know them." A mutual friend, Gaspard Rusanganwa, an assistant bourgmestre of Ngoma, the urban commune of Butare, helped to cement the friendship. Rusanganwa lived next door to the monastery; the plot had been given to him by the nuns, according to Rekeraho. Rekeraho is now in prison, accused of genocide, and has given a lengthy and frank account of his meetings with the nuns and of their involvement in the killings at Sovu.

Rekeraho was the representative of the Democratic Republican Movement (MDR) in the commune of Huye. He organised meetings to plan the genocide all over the commune of Huye and toured the area spreading a message of hatred. His activities were well-known. Jean-Baptiste Muvunyi, the local councillor, described how Rekeraho prepared the ground for the killings in Sovu.

Rekeraho told me that it was absolutely essential to hunt down and kill all the *Inyenzi* because they were accomplices of the RPF who had a plan to exterminate all the Hutus, after they had killed their president. Not a single Tutsi was killed here in our area during the first few days following Habyarimana's death, but none dared spend the night at home. They were all spending the night in the bush or banana groves. Rekeraho had in fact organised the militia and they were meeting daily and going from cellule to cellule, counting the Tutsis and intimidating them. On 15 April, they started burning the houses of Tutsis in Maraba, a commune that borders Gikongoro. The bourgmestre called a public meeting on 17 April in the market of Gako. The Tutsis present told him about their fears, but the bourgmestre could no longer control the young Hutus led by Rekeraho.

The refugees who had gone to the monastery saw Rekeraho almost immediately they arrived. Augustin Ngirinshuti, a 36-year-old farmer originally from Nyanyumba in Gisenyi, spent the critical weeks of April in the Sovu monastery. He had come with his wife, Marcelline Nyirakimonyo, to Ruhashya in Butare to visit his in-laws. On 6 April, Augustin and his wife decided to visit the nuns; they knew them because the Benedictine order has a house near their home in Gisenyi. Although he is Hutu and could have left the monastery, Augustin was fearful that his Tutsi wife would be killed at the roadblocks, so the couple decided to remain and work in the monastery's kitchen. Augustin said the purpose of Rekeraho's first visit was to count and identify the Tutsis in the monastery.

Warrant Officer Rekeraho arrived at the monastery with Gaspard Rusanganwa. Rekeraho asked the nuns to draw up separate lists of the refugees and those who were attending a meeting there. I heard the Tutsis saying angrily that Gertrude had asked them to leave the monastery so that the militia would not attack it.

Saying that he was "willing to testify in the government's courts, at Arusha and before God", Augustin commented on the frequency of Rekeraho's meetings with the nuns.

I also saw Rekeraho coming round all the time, talking only to Gertrude and Kizito. Kizito was always going out with Rekeraho. I don't know where they went but it was no secret that they were frequently together. I often saw her leave with Rekeraho and other militiamen, and spend many hours outside the monastery. She often used to chat to the militiamen. I even heard Kizito say that she had been oppressed for a long time, and the time had now come for her to take revenge.[19]

After the killings had begun in earnest throughout the préfecture, on 20 April, Rekeraho came back to the monastery. On this occasion, Sr. Gertrude lent him an ambulance which belonged to the health centre. Rekeraho used the nuns' ambulance to carry out the genocide, according to many residents of Sovu and according to his own testimony. Joseph Sengoga, 47 and a welder, has been

---

[18] Rekeraho fled to Zaire in July 1994. He was arrested in Kisangani, Democratic Republic of Congo (DRC) on 4 September 1997 and brought back to Rwanda.

[19] Interviewed in Ruhashya, 2 June 1999.

detained in Karubanda Prison in Butare since 2 May 1998, charged with involvement in the genocide. He lived close to the monastery and he spoke of the nuns' gift to Rekeraho.

> Rekeraho toured everywhere during the genocide. He led the militia and some ex-soldiers, and used to drive the nuns' cream-coloured ambulance, using a microphone inside it to call on all the Hutus to kill the Tutsis. The nuns had given him the vehicle so that he would accompany them into town when they did their shopping. He was the only person in Sovu who had transport. He often went to see the nuns. Rekeraho acted as though he owned the region, almost like a bourgmestre.[20]

Rekeraho discovered just how sympathetic Sr. Gertrude had become to the militiamen's cause when he met with the nuns at the home of the assistant bourgmestre, Gaspard Rusanganwa. That day the nuns offered to lend both Rekeraho and Rusanganwa vehicles which belonged to the monastery.

> Between 20-21 April the Tutsis continued to flee to the monasteries of Sovu and Gihindamuyaga. On 20 April, between 5:00 p.m. and 7:30 p.m., I went to see my friend Gaspard Rusanganwa, the assistant bourgmestre of Ngoma, who lived next to the monastery. Gertrude Mukangango and Julienne Kizito joined me there. We began talking about Habyarimana's death. I didn't like Habyarimana, although I didn't want him to die. We were sad that Habyarimana had been shot down by the *Inyenzi*. It was then that Sr. Gertrude said we must avenge him.

Sr. Gertrude said she would help Rekeraho and Rusanganwa "avenge" Habyarimana's assassination; she was apparently influenced by the words of the then President, Sindikubwabo.

> After these comments about the President's death, Rusanganwa explained what Sindikubwabo had meant the day before when he said that the residents of Butare had become "*Ntibindeba.*" Gertrude then said that Sindikubwabo was in fact right because until then, the Hutus of Butare had done nothing. For example, she said she was surprised that the Hutus had not yet killed the large number of Tutsis in the monastery. She criticised the weakness of the residents of Butare, with the exception of the people of Maraba. She also said that she was afraid of being killed by the Tutsi nuns in her monastery, and said that she thought there were too many of them. She told us: "You see all these Tutsis who are at the monastery? If you don't do anything, they could kill me. It is possible that you will not even get to see my corpse!" She asked us to follow the example of the people of Maraba who had already started to kill the Tutsis and to eat their cows.
> During that evening, the two nuns suggested giving me the minibus, the beige-coloured Hiace, so that I could ensure their security. They also offered Gaspard Rusanganwa a Volkswagen, and promised to supply all the petrol I needed, so that I could drive around freely.
> We left Rusanganwa's place at about 7:30 p.m. I left my motorbike there and went with the nuns to get the keys for the Hiace; but our friend Gaspard said that he was too ill to drive the Volkswagen. He told me later in Zaire that he had been afraid of an attack by the Tutsis in the monastery as that was right next to his house.

Rekeraho's conversation with Gertrude and Kizito on 20 April was the turning point in their relationship. It was, he said, "on 20 April 1994 that I became intimate with the nuns, that I exchanged confidences with them."

But although it was obvious that Gertrude and Kizito were in touch with the militia, the other nuns were given a false sense of security by Kizito's reports. Marie-Bernard Kayitesi, who was a nun at Sovu but has since left the Church, remembered how she assured the refugees they had nothing to fear.

> When she came back to the community, she would tell us that neither the monastery nor the health centre would be attacked. She even went to the health centre and told the Tutsi refugees that, if they wanted to save their lives, they must stay there and gave her guarantee that the monastery and health centre would be safe from attack. I just cannot forgive her for that, because all she wanted was to make

---

[20] Interviewed in Ngoma, 11 May 1999.

sure the refugees stayed together to make the militia's task of wiping them out easier. Perhaps, if she had not said that, the refugees might have left the health centre to seek refuge elsewhere.[21]

Starving the Refugees

In the same way that she denied the refugees shelter when there was room inside the monastery, Sr. Gertrude deprived them of food when she had plenty of supplies. The Caritas office of the Diocese of Butare had sent rice to the monastery, but Sr. Gertrude locked the supplies in the storeroom of the health centre and refused to give any to the refugees.

Annonciata Mukagasana, 31, was an applicant[22] at the monastery; today she works as a nurse at a hospital in Butare. She described Sr. Gertrude as "heartless" because she would not give the refugees any food unless they were able to pay for it. She commented: "Many of the Sisters were shocked by such behaviour."[23] Marie-Bernard Kayitesi added:

> To the surprise of all the nuns in Sovu, Gertrude flatly refused to distribute the food to the refugees, even though they were starving. She quite simply refused to unlock the storeroom.

Many of the refugees had brought their livestock with them, but the cows were looted by the militiamen. According to Marie-Bernard, Sr. Gertrude even refused the refugees access to their own food.

As the refugees' situation deteriorated, a Polish Carmelite nun who managed the health centre, Sr. Marie Paul, had returned to the Parish of Rugango to fetch some additional sacks of rice. The rice was stored at the health centre. After the first grenades exploded on the 18th, the people who had been at the health centre scattered in different directions, including the person who had the key to the room where the rice had been stored. Consolée Mukeshimana, who worked at the health centre asked Sr. Gertrude for a spare key. A nun who was there at the time remembered how Sr. Gertrude refused to give anyone the key, "although it was only to get supplies of rice that she herself had not bought."

Sr. Kizito also opposed even the smallest gesture of kindness to the refugees. Juliette Mukangango was sitting in the courtyard and witnessed how she deprived children of food.

> Kizito took the youngest children somewhere behind us, and made them sit on the lawn. A workman called Jean Sebuhinyori picked some guavas to give to the children. Kizito refused and removed the basket.

Sr. Gertrude and Sr. Julienne exploited the refugees' hunger in order to calculate the number of refugees. On Tuesday 19 April, a monastery worker was sent to make a list of all those who had gathered at the monastery. The nuns said it would be used to determine how much food would be needed. But once the census had been taken, the Mother Superior did not make any attempt to feed the refugees, as Consolée Mukeshimana pointed out.

> The Benedictine Sisters of Sovu didn't make any gesture of assistance towards us during our entire stay there. The only thing they did was to send us a watchman at their monastery, Jean Sebuhinyori, to take a census supposedly so that they could feed us. But it was a lie. They did not give us anything to eat.

Lambert Nsabimana remarked that there was no shortage of food.

---

[21] Interviewed in Kigali, 22 October 1996.

[22] Applicants, known as *postulants*, are young women who have shown an interest in becoming nuns. They live with nuns in a monastery or convent after which they take their first vows and become novices.

[23] Interviewed in Ngoma, 1 June 1999.

They did not give us any food—even to the young and sick—when they were hardly short of supplies. And yet they had the names listed, [allegedly] for that reason.

Séraphine Mukamana and Lucie Mugorewase were among the crowd of refugees and they are also convinced that Sr. Gertrude never had any intention of feeding them, that she was simply "lying." Juliette Mukangango said Sr. Kizito was involved in counting the refugees and that she wanted detailed information about each of them.

She suggested listing by families, starting with Karuhaya and Karido cellules. She gave the lists to Cassien Karido and to Sebuhinyori's son, Kabera, a university student. We stayed there, but had nothing to eat.

While the refugees were being counted, Sr. Kizito was reassuring the refugees. Renata Gatesi recalled their confidence in her, and the disappointment that followed.

Kizito told me not to worry because we were well protected. She asked us to draw up a list of our names, family by family. This was supposedly so that we could be provided with food. As she too came from this area, we thought she was genuinely concerned about us. We waited in vain for the food. That Tuesday night, Sr. Fortunata and Mpambara brought us some porridge, but secretly.

Marie-Goretti Mbateye said that "it became more and more difficult to look into the eyes of people who were starving."

Kizito had told us that they were taking the census so that they could know our exact number in order to feed us. Once the papers had been completed, they were given to Jean Sebuhinyori. He took them to the nuns. We waited for food, but in vain. We received nothing from the nuns, not even one banana for the babies. Really nothing. I didn't have children there, but it pained me to see the children of my family and others cry from hunger. From time to time, some of the people who were not afraid went into the surrounding areas in search of some sweet potatoes, potatoes or bananas. But there were so many of us that we needed a lot of food. But no-one gave us any.

Ruth Mugorewase suggested that the purpose of the exercise was to allay the refugees' suspicions.

Kizito lied to us, saying that Caritas was going to give us food, which was the reason why she wanted to know our number. Every moment the number was growing. While Kizito was counting, Gertrude and the bourgmestre went to Butare to bring back soldiers who had many guns. The soldiers' vehicle came back with Gertrude; they saw what the situation was. Kizito advised them to leave us for a while, so that we could die of hunger. The soldier said: "It's a good idea; the police and the population are guarding them so that no-one can get out of the centre."

Many refugees arrived at the monastery with serious wounds. Sr. Cécile Mukasekuru, who was training to be a nurse, was on placement at Sovu health centre during the holidays. But she refused to dress the refugees' wounds, saying they were poor and could not pay her. According to Marie-Bernard, "She also said they were wicked people who had killed President Habyarimana." Sr. Cécile Mukasekuru is a close relative of Sr. Gertrude. For medical care, the wounded refugees were dependent on Sr. Solange Uwanyirigira, also studying to be a nurse. However, as the security situation deteriorated, her own vulnerability as a Tutsi made it increasingly difficult for her to leave the monastery and tend to the medical needs of the refugees at the health centre.

The First Attempt: 21 April

"The plan was to kill all of them."

Emmanuel Rekeraho said he was at home on 21 April when Pierre Rushyana, one of Sovu's leading militiamen, and four young men came to his house. They told him that the Tutsi refugees had attacked the assistant bourgmestre, Gaspard Rusanganwa, and left one man dead. It was a lie, but it had the desired effect. Rekeraho gave details of the punitive expedition he organised, using the vehicle which Sr. Gertrude had given him.

> I jumped into the nuns' minibus and went to see Karekezi, Rusanganwa's father. I found Gaspard by his parents' kitchen. We had a brief conversation. A lot of Hutus arrived. We took our arms and went after the Tutsis. We had whistles and drums, and wore feathers in our hair. Kamanayo [a soldier], Muvunyi [councillor of Sovu], Gaspard and I led this expedition. The Tutsis had defied us, and we decided that we had to prove to them that we were stronger, that we outnumbered them. But I must tell you that we were afraid of the Tutsis because, up until then, they had fought back very well. Unfortunately for us, despite our numbers, a lot of people deserted the battle to go and have a beer or to loot the Tutsis' cattle and belongings. That element weakened us.

Rekeraho also described the state in which they found the refugees.

> As for the Tutsis they seemed very tired and hungry. I don't think that Sr. Gertrude and Sr. Kizito had bothered to give them anything to eat, after the way that they had been talking about them at Rusanganwa's the evening of 20 April. But they were determined to fight us with everything that they had at their disposal. That day we managed to drive them right inside the monastery. Afterwards, I ordered the young Hutus, the interahamwe although I don't like the term, to surround the monastery and the health centre, so that not a single Tutsi should escape us. After that, I went to have a beer.

On the way, Rekeraho had an encounter with two senior military commanders.

> I saw about ten soldiers in uniform heading towards the health centre coming from ESO [the Junior Officers' School in Ngoma], so I followed them. Sometime later, Lt.Col. Muvunyi, the commander of ESO and of operations in Butare and Gikongoro, also came, together with Major Cyriaque Habyarabatume [head of the gendarmerie in Butare]. They ordered these soldiers to get all the Tutsis out of the health centre. We took them nearly as far as Maraba's bar. We killed those who tried to escape on the spot. We insulted them and called them all the names in the book, to humiliate and annoy them. The plan was to kill all of them. But as the evening drew on, we could see that it would be difficult, if not impossible, to kill such a large number of people, so we told them to go back to the health centre.

Rekeraho said that "the older people went home, leaving the interahamwe to surround the monastery and the health centre that evening." In common with many other survivors, Consolée Mukeshimana remembered that Pierre Rushyana of MDR-Power and the twin sons of Baributsa— Gakuru and Gato—were leading the killers.

> When they threw grenades, we dispersed. We took different directions but many people walked towards the monastery.

It was the day Lambert Nsabimana decided to take his wife away from the monastery.

> On Thursday the 21st, the whole area from Kukinyana to Gihindamuyaga was full of people. They were acting like lunatics. It was too late for me to rejoin the Tutsis. It was all over. I called Ruvebana over and asked him to go and find my wife. I was near the monastery. The Hutus there were in such a rage that I realised they would massacre the Tutsis. When my wife got out, I took her to Rushyana's house. He was a close colleague of Rekeraho's, so she was in a place of safety. In the meantime, Sr. Kizito was busy dispossessing the Tutsis of their clubs and *massues*.

The commotion could be heard at the monastery. Régine recalled the fear and panic it provoked.

At 9:00 a.m. on 21 April we heard noise, whistling, shouting and chanting. We were told that it was the interahamwe on their way to kill people at the heath centre. We immediately went to the hostelry and started praying. We recited the rosary with our families and the other refugees. We were waiting for our turn, and preparing ourselves by praying. From the hostelry, we could hear hand grenades exploding and gunfire.

Burning, Stoning and Hacking the Refugees to Death
The Massacre at Sovu Health Centre, 22 April 1994

"Above all, the killers were looking for men. I don't think a single Tutsi man escaped."

There were between 5,000-6,000 Tutsis at the health centre by 22 April. Except for the nuns' relatives, all the Tutsis had been forced out of the monastery. Weakened and exposed, they listened to the sound of gunfire and grenades from nearby Gihindamuyaga and from Butare town. Domatile Mukabanza described their situation as one of "total desolation." A massacre at the Benedictine monastery in Gihindamuyaga, only about a kilometre and a half from the monastery, heightened the refugees' fears, but the gendarmes at the monastery had continued to tell the refugees that "nothing was going to happen."

On Friday 22 April, around 8:00 a.m., the monastery was surrounded by interahamwe, soldiers, communal policemen and local civilians. The gendarmes who had been sent to protect the monastery joined the attackers, leaving the refugees with no defences. The nuns in the monastery were told what to expect by Sr. Kizito, but she also assured them that nothing could be done to prevent it.

> She said: "Don't be surprised if you see the militia exploding grenades at the Sovu health centre." We were frightened and asked her to do everything she could to calm the militiamen. At about 1:00 p.m., Kizito told us nothing could be done to stop them throwing their grenades. We soon saw Kizito's words come true. At about 3:00 p.m., the murderers blew up the Sovu health centre. They threw their grenades and used their weapons to exterminate all the refugees at the health centre. They killed until the following day. Many of the survivors were badly wounded and their limbs amputated.

Rekeraho has admitted his full part in the massacre. He said he had a drink and then went to the health centre with the intention of killing all the Tutsis there. He described the horror of the massacre.

> I killed children, old men and women. We had become like animals, myself included. I took pity on no-one, not even my friends. What we did is beyond belief. I don't know if we can be forgiven. They had already begun killing by the time I reached the health centre; they were smashing their way in, throwing in hand-grenades. Even the policeman, François-Xavier Munyeshyaka, who was supposed to protect the nuns, was killing people. There were a lot of Lt.Col. Muvunyi's soldiers, and gendarmes taking part in the killing, together with the interahamwe. The poor Tutsis were throwing bricks at us. But what use were bricks and stones against fire arms? Women and children were groaning and screaming. I find it hard to recall such horrors. We really did behave like animals. I feel entirely responsible for what I did. I will never deny my participation in the genocide of the Tutsis.

"Many of us threw hand-grenades from behind the wall. When we got inside, it was horrible to see how we used machetes to execute our neighbours, people with whom we had shared everything, even our blood. There were defenceless, weak people there, and we could not look them in the eye."

According to Rekeraho, the refugees tried to defend themselves, but the forces of the genocide were stronger.

> Without the help of the soldiers and gendarmes, it would have been impossible for us to kill everyone all by ourselves. Their support was critical. There were so many Tutsis and they were quite good at defending themselves despite their lack of means. First Sergeant Nsabimana, together with a dozen soldiers and two gendarmes, entered the health centre to give encouragement to the interahamwe who were unable to crush the resistance of the Tutsis.

Séraphine remembered the scale of the assault.

It was as if all the men, women and children had come to kill us. Almost all the communal policemen of Huye were there, as well as retired soldiers of Huye, armed with grenades and guns.

Juliette Mukangango had sent away her three children before the killing got underway. Their deceased father was Hutu and she knew they had a better chance of surviving elsewhere. She spoke of the role of women in the massacre on 22 April.

We heard whistles, drumming and chanting. The girls and women were in front. We began to pray; and they began their "work." They shot, stabbed and stoned us without mercy. They even threw pepper [tear gas] at us. Gaspard Rusanganwa, Rekeraho, Jean-Baptiste Muvunyi and Jonas Ndayisaba were there. They went to see the nuns afterwards, and then came back with them. I heard Rekeraho tell the militia that their Sisters were coming to help them (*Bashiki bacu baratugo boste*). He also said, "Kill them all, every last one, so that we will forget what the Tutsis ever looked like." At that moment, I was hiding in a bush and pretended to be dead. Before they died, I heard Tutsis screaming "We're being exterminated."

Domatile Mukabanza was among the refugees. She remembers seeing Sr. Kizito in the midst of the huge group of assaillants.

Amongst them I saw Sister Julienne, the daughter of Semanyana of Sovu. She was in the middle talking to her brothers who were amongst the attackers and she was giving them a list. No doubt, it was the list of the Tutsi workers and refugees who remained in the monastery. Next to Sr. Kizito was a man called Karangwa from Gihindamuyaga who was dancing in front of her with a spear in his hand.

Domatile said the killing continued until around 5:00 p.m. There was no doubt that the killers' principal target was men.

The gendarmes arrived [around 5:00 p.m.] and stopped the killing. They grouped us together, saying that they were going to assure our security. But when we arrived on the Butare-Gikongoro road, they forced us to sit down on the grass. Some of them wanted to finish us off. There was not a single man amongst us. I don't think a single Tutsi man had escaped. They forced us to go back to the health centre where we spent the night in the middle of the corpses.

Although she was married to a Hutu and had six children, Marie-Goretti Mbateye decided to leave her family at home and to hide at the health centre. She explained her reasoning: "I didn't have any guarantee that they would not come to kill or rape me in front of my children if I stayed at home." When she heard deafening noise on the morning of the 22nd, she turned to one of the policemen at the monastery, Xavier Nsanzabera, shortly before he joined the ranks of the killers. He told her that "they should have no fear."

I went outside to join the people who were warming themselves in the sun in order to find out where this noise was coming from. These men said that we were surrounded. They asked us to gather stones. The women began to collect the stones and bricks for the men to throw. The militia came towards us, in huge numbers, from all directions. They threw stones at us to provoke us and to see if we were going to react. Maybe they thought that some of us had hidden weapons.

The men and boys used the stones and bricks, but it was no defence against guns and grenades.

The men tried to put up a fight with their stones. We heard the explosion of a grenade which made us lie down. There was such panic! Before we got up, there was another explosion which reinforced our fear. Next to me there was a young man who had been hit on the head by a grenade. He was groaning. I went to see my mother inside the centre; she asked me to give her water to drink. The others advised me to pour the water on her bleeding head, which is what I did.

Some men also fled the outside and came inside the centre. The militia arrived; they killed the people who were outside. But there were not only militiamen; there were also soldiers, gendarmes and communal policemen. Some people managed to hide in the garage, others in the outlying buildings, some inside the health centre and others in the bush.

Most of them died that day.

The militia reached the gate. There was a great confusion. In a loud voice, Jean-Chrysostome, the son of councillor Jean-Baptiste Muvunyi, asked all those who had Hutu blood in their veins to get out. At that moment, I saw an interahamwe called Isaac Mugoyi slit the throat of Nyamaswa who was lying on the ground. Mugoyi then searched his pockets for money, stripped him and took his clothes. I saw Rekeraho, Rusanganwa, Mutabaruka, Rushyana and his son and many others. They were killing with machetes, grenades and *massues*, but also with bullets. There was pandemonium. I also saw another militia carrying a branch from which the head of Dominique Hategeka was suspended. There was a massive number of Tutsis which explains why they didn't finish killing them in a hurry.

The pace of the slaughter increased once Rekeraho took charge.

Rekeraho, Rusanganwa and Jonas Ndayisaba entered the centre with many others to kill. They did not spare anyone, not even babies. I saw babies suckling their mothers who had just been killed.

Before they reached Marie-Goretti and her companions, Rekeraho told the killers to spare Tutsi women married to Hutus. One of Marie-Goretti's nephews, whose father was Hutu, took advantage of the offer and came out of hiding. "He had to trample on the corpses because there were so many of them." Marie-Goretti's brother, Callixte Kalisa, went to ask the militiaman, Jean-Chrysostome Muvunyi, to allow Marie-Goretti to leave the health centre as her husband was Hutu.

Jean-Chrysostome asked him to get nearer so that they could explain to him how I might escape. The poor man went. A militiaman cut his head off on the spot. We fled from instinct, preferring to die outside instead of waiting for the walls of the buildings to crumble on us.

Renata Gatesi and a companion had gone to pick avocados when they saw militiamen approaching the health centre on the morning of the 22nd. She described how "their bodies and minds came to be damaged."

Immediately after that we heard drums. We ran straight back to the health centre to warn the others. We used our wraps to collect bricks and stones. Then a lot of militiamen arrived. Some men had been outside enjoying the sunshine. They killed them first. The policemen who were supposed to be protecting us began to shoot at us. We tried throwing bricks and stones at them. They threw grenades inside. Many children who were in there with me died, including Murangwa and Eugénie. My sister, Mukabutera, was hit in the shoulders. I was hit by shrapnel in the ribs and my right arm. Athanase Biseruka's son had a leg blown off and someone else was blown to pieces in front of me.

When I got hit, I made my way towards them so that they would finish me off. That was when they threw a stone at me that hit my upper lip. You can see the scar. I felt dizzy and was bleeding badly. My sister, Mukabutera, also wanted to go to the killers but I stopped her. They went on killing and killing for a long time, sparing no-one, not even the babies. I saw a militiaman kill my father with a club.

Renata ended her testimony by saying that "our minds will never be healed."

Consolée Mukeshimana's house was located close to the monastery. When she saw the large and well-armed crowd approach the health centre she ran inside. Through her window she could see the unrelenting slaughter. But then she was forced out of her home.

The communal policemen included Joseph Murwanashyaka; Cassien Uwizeyimana; Xavier Nsababera; Joseph Bizimana and Munyankindi. The soldiers included Pascal Karekezi and Kamanayo.

The massacre started at about 9:00 a.m. The killing continued until 5:00 p.m. However, at about 2:00 p.m., the house I was in was set on fire by petrol and I left it. When I got outside, I was shot at. I was not wounded. But I felt dizzy and I fell to the ground. I lay in the middle of the victims who were on the ground. I stayed stretched out but I could hear everything. Towards 5:30 p.m., six gendarmes arrived and stopped the killings. They told the killers to loot only.

Consolée heard the gendarmes telling women and girls that they would protect them. So she got up to join them.

The courtyard of the centre was strewn with corpses. You couldn't find anywhere to put your feet. They made us come down. When we arrived on the Butare-Gikongoro road, they told us to sit down. They took up their positions and we thought it was all over for us. But they spoke amongst themselves and they made us go back to the health centre in a hurry. It was already late. We left once again for the health centre, in the middle of the bodies of our families who had been killed. During the night, I left because I saw that the killers were going to come back the following day.

Realising that the killers might return the following day, Consolée left the monastery that night. But many people were too badly injured to make an escape. Some of the survivors stumbled into the monastery to seek help from the nuns. Marie-Bernard described the state they were in.

Many were seriously wounded and had lost arms and legs.

Burned Alive in the Garage of the Health Centre

One of the most horrific incidents in the massacre of 22 April was at the garage of the health centre. Some 700 men, women and children were crammed inside the garage, which has a staircase leading to a cellar. Surrounded by armed attackers, they locked the garage from the inside. Testimonies from witnesses emphasise the key role of Sr. Kizito in ensuring that the garage became a death trap. It was she, the refugees say, who provided the petrol with which the militia burned many of the refugees alive.

First the militia tried to force all the refugees out of the garage, according to Séraphine Mukamana who was inside. But the certainty that they would be killed once they left the garage held the refugees back.

They shot into the door but we refused to leave, despite the holes these bullets made in the door. In particular, it was the communal policeman called Xavier who shot into us. Through these [bullet] holes, we could see who was shooting and the faces of some of the killers.

The génocidaires realised that the refugees were determined to hold out and they decided to burn down the garage, so they would either be forced out or would die inside. They locked the door with a padlock so no one could escape and then doused the building in petrol. Séraphine described the effect; she and her sister Adelice were inside, but both survived.

The heat and the smoke overcame us and forced us to stop pushing the door. But the fire hadn't yet reached the inside of the garage, although the heat and the smoke had. As there were far too many of us in the garage for its size, many of the refugees suffocated to death. There were about 700 of us. Some of the men were looking for a way out by opening the door. But the génocidaires had locked us in from the outside. And so these refugees used their machetes to make an exit in the door. But the door was solid. Even so, they managed to make a small escape route. However, all the refugees who went out through this gap were immediately killed by the génocidaires outside. A lot of refugees preferred to go out and die from the blows of the interahamwe rather than by suffocation.

Séraphine somehow managed to avoid the flames. But when the militia realised that the petrol had not killed everyone, Séraphine said, they entered the garage, armed with machetes, *massues*, spears and axes, and she was beaten unconscious. She woke the following morning, surrounded by the charred corpses of her fellow refugees.

Séraphine's mother, Vénéranda Mukankusi, watched as the preparations to burn down the garage got underway. She said Sr. Kizito was closely involved with the killings.

> I was neither among the killers nor among the victims. I just watched. I saw Sr. Kizito with seven litre jerrycans full of petrol. She distributed them to the killers. Since the refugees were not in the courtyard, but had locked themselves inside the buildings, they poured the petrol on the building and set it alight. Sr. Kizito was still there and she gave several jerrycans of petrol. My other children were killed that day. But my two daughters had taken refuge in the garage. I believed that they had been burned down there.

Vénéranda said she left the site "in a state of madness." When she reached the home of the friend who had given her shelter, she said she "could do nothing else except cry out for help." Her distress moved one militiaman who returned to the garage and rescued Séraphine.

The killers did not think the petrol was burning the refugees fast enough. Ruth Mugorewase was also in the garage. She heard Sr. Kizito organising a way to spread the fire.

> Kizito realised there were people in the garage. She told the peasants to bring some dry grass to use for burning the people in the garage with petrol. Rekeraho, a soldier, helped Kizito to pour the petrol through the holes and all around the garage. They lit up the whole garage until nearly everyone was dead. I threw myself into a pile of food stocks.

When the killings were over, Ruth overheard Sr. Kizito discussing the refugees' fate with Sr. Gertrude and Rekeraho.

> I heard Kizito and Gertrude talking about looking at the list to see if everyone was dead so that they could go and make a list of the Tutsi Sisters because their turn had not yet come. Rekeraho said: "We are tired and it is night-time; we must rest and come back tomorrow. If there are still people who are alive, our Sisters will help us." They left.

Ruth left the garage during the night, hiding in the bush. Unfortunately, she was discovered, beaten and thrown in a mass grave in Sovu. She crawled out during the night and made her way to the town of Butare where she stayed until the end of the genocide.

Vestine witnessed the fire. She was crouching nearby when Sr. Kizito went in search of petrol and dry grass to intensify the burning.

> Kizito brought a jerrycan to the garage, full of people. She was with a soldier I didn't know. I was right beside them; they also took dry grass and they burned the whole of the garage building.

Disoriented with fear, Alphonsine Mukamudenge's family had separated. Her husband had hidden in the garage, where he was killed, and three of her four children died in the health centre. She left the health centre and sought cover in a nearby bush, from where she saw Sr. Kizito arranging her husband's murder.

> When the soldiers and the communal policemen were throwing grenades and shooting, Kizito went to get petrol to burn the people who were in the garage. Kizito and Warrant Officer Rekeraho brought dry grass with a jerrycan of petrol. They burned down the whole garage. Gertrude and Kizito became more notorious than the soldiers. Even the soldiers were surprised to see the Sisters involved in killing the Tutsis.

Marie-Goretti Mbateye, injured by shrapnel, ran out of the health centre after her brother was killed in front of her. But there was more suffering in store for her as she lay on a patch of grass near the garage.

I saw Rekeraho and Rusanganwa holding two jerrycans. They were accompanied by Kizito and Gertrude. I saw them clearly. The interahamwe were digging the area around the garage. Others went to look for straw. I remember Alimasi; there were others with him. They poured the petrol on the straw which they threw into the garage and into the hole they had just dug.

The garage began to burn. The people who had not been killed by the fire or by asphyxiation came out. My younger sister, Bernadette Mukantwari, was amongst them. She came out with a leg that had been burnt. She was incapable of running; she fell in the middle of the health centre.

Mindful of Rekeraho's order that Tutsi women married to Hutus should not be touched, the killers allowed Marie-Goretti to walk home.

Before leaving, I saw the two nuns walking around in the centre looking at all the corpses. Kizito was complaining that the Tutsis were very bad because they had torn up their bank notes before dying.

Renata had made her way out of the health centre by the time the killers had turned their attention to the garage.

They discovered that there were a lot of people in the garage. They were shouting about it. They said that they would have to burn them because they had barricaded the garage door. I was with my sister, Mukabutera, in the health centre kitchen. There were a lot of people in the garage. Rekeraho asked Gaspard to go and get some petrol from the nuns. They left with Jonas Ndayisaba. They were talking at the top of their voices to make themselves heard because of the noise from the explosions and people crying out. They came back with Kizito and Gertrude, and two jerrycans of petrol. Rekeraho said: "Our Sisters have come to our aid". (*Bashiki bacu baratugo botse*).

Rekeraho gave the petrol to Vincent Byomboka who had some straw. Vincent started pouring the petrol over the garage, and his colleagues joined in. Almost choked to death, some of the Tutsis tried to get out by hacking at the door with pruning knives which they had managed to hide when the nuns took away all their defensive weapons. I saw Cansilde Mukamushongore stoned to death. Ngaboniza was cut to pieces. Bernadette Mukantwari came out with one leg on fire. I saw Kabirigi with his body all on fire as he ran. Many people died inside the garage.

We were still hiding in our little corner. The militia were bent on killing and looting, and had no idea we were still alive. They kept on killing until the evening. Kizito came back, walked all round the bodies and said: "See how wicked these Tutsis are! They've torn up their banknotes so the Hutus can't use them! They should all be killed!"

We were lying among the bodies, pretending to be dead. Rekeraho was there too. I heard him tell the militia: "Report very early tomorrow morning, because you'll be working at the commune office as well as afterwards."

Consolée Mukeshimana also saw Sr. Kizito collaborating with the militia.

Before the beginning of the attack, I saw a nun from Sovu, Julienne Kizito, in the middle of the génocidaires. Next to her was a jerrycan of petrol and she had a list in her hands. She gave this jerrycan of petrol to a criminal whom I was not able to recognise.

Josée Mukarwego was one of many Hutu women placed in an impossible situation in April. Her husband was Tutsi and the couple sought refuge at the health centre with their children. On 22 April, her husband and three of her seven children were hacked to pieces by men she knew well. Her oldest son, Edouard, was killed soon afterwards in the garage fire. Josée witnessed Edouard's death and that of her mother-in-law who was also in the garage.

My oldest son, wounded by an arrow, had hidden in the garage. I saw that his intestines were hanging out. The génocidaires had set the garage on fire. But the garage had not burned down completely. Nevertheless, the smoke killed people and forced others to leave; they were battered to death outside. My mother-in-law was killed down there in front of my eyes. She pulled at her clothes that the killers wanted to wrench from her before they killed her. They killed her and afterwards took her clothes.

The burning of the garage was followed by an attack upon a worker at the monastery, Gérard Kabirigi. Again Sr. Kizito was involved. Josée lived nearby and knew the staff at the monastery. She recognised Sr. Kizito helping the interahamwe kill Kabirigi.

> I saw the daughter of Semanya, that is Sr. Julienne Kizito. She had a seven-litre jerrycan of petrol. Kabirigi, a Tutsi worker at the health centre, was also there, in this confusion. You can still see his house in this area. She gave the petrol to an interahamwe from her family called Niyonsenga. He poured the petrol over Kabirigi and set him on fire. Kabirigi ran while burning. Kizito was there and it really was her who had just given the petrol. Me too, I was there. It was the day that my family died.

Other witnesses have also accused Kizito of providing the petrol used to set Gérard Kabirigi on fire. Alice Mukankundiye was near the scene when he was set alight. Alice knew Kabirigi because he was engaged to her younger sister.

> Sr. Kizito provided the petrol used to burn down the health centre's garage. That same petrol was also used to burn alive my younger sister's fiancée, a man called Gérard Kabirigi. When he was thrown out of the monastery, Kabirigi headed for the health centre. Kizito, who had a small can of petrol with her, passed this to a militiaman who immediately poured the contents over Kabirigi. The militiaman then threw a lit match at him, setting him alight. Kabirigi was nothing more than a human torch as he ran through the forest; he finally died the bush.

When African Rights visited the monastery in July 1995, the charred rags of the people burned alive at the garage on 22 April covered the ground. The evidence was still visible during subsequent visits in November 1995 and on many other occasions in 1996/7. Today, the garage has been cleaned up and whitewashed. But the victims have not been forgotten.

Sr. Kizito has a particular responsibility for causing the deaths of the people who were inside the garage in one of the most painful ways imaginable. The fire will always be remembered by the survivors of Sovu as one of the most effective methods used by the militia and one of the most cruel acts to have been committed by Sr. Kizito. The complicity of Sr. Gertrude in the terrible violence of 22 April is confirmed by the statement she is said to have made to the nuns that evening. According to Marie-Bernard Kayitesi.

> In the evening, Gertrude told us that the murderers had informed her that it would be the nuns' turn next day. She said: "Those of you who are going to die, prepare yourselves. Put on your habits. This is how it is in life. It's only natural that the refugees at the health centre have been killed. They had been digging graves for the Hutus."

In fact, the murder of the Tutsi nuns' relatives in the monastery would only come two days later. First the militiamen were most concerned with eliminating any survivors of the massacre of 22 April, in looting its spoils and in clearing up the evidence. In all these tasks they were assisted by Sr. Gertrude and Sr. Kizito.

Very early on the morning of 23 April, Sr. Gertrude insisted that all the nuns leave the monastery, telling them that it would otherwise be "their turn to be killed." Three of the nuns who had hidden their relatives there—Scholastique, Fortunata and Bénédicte—decided to remain with their family members. Annonciata Mukagasana described an incident that took place shortly before they left the monastery.

> Gertrude thought that Sr. Bernadette had hidden our driver, Anastase. She insulted Bernadette, calling her a liar, and saying she should take off her veil and leave the monastery, rather than continue to lie.

Marie-Bernard described what they saw on the journey to Ngoma.

> We saw bodies everywhere; they looked like empty clothes, scattered on the ground. It was a terrible sight. I kept thinking this was the end of the world the Bible spoke of.

The garage at the health centre after the fire

Eugénie Mukagatera said Sr. Gertrude made sure they did not travel alone.

> Gertrude took the wheel and made us first pass the home of the bourgmestre of Huye, Ruremesha, who accompanied us to the Parish of Ngoma.

They were well-protected. Marie-Bernard mentioned the génocidaires that Sr. Gertrude chose as their escorts.

> There was a communal policeman called Xavier who was supposed to be protecting the monastery, though he played an active part in the massacre of 22 April. I myself saw him open fire on the refugees that day. But he was the one who went with us in the monastery's Mazda when Gertrude drove us to Ngoma.
> First, we went to the commune office in Huye and Sr. Gertrude asked the bourgmestre, Jonathan Ruremesha, to escort us to the bishopric. He said that he would help us to get to Ngoma. He took some of the nuns in his car, because there was not room for us all in the Mazda.

Displaying a Tutsi identity card at roadblocks was usually the prelude to death and Sr. Gertrude could not have been oblivious to the danger. She had, in fact, warned the nuns herself about ID cards on the evening of the 19th when Annonciata said she told them that "if anyone wanted to know our identity, we should not show our cards, but say instead that we are all Christians." But by the 23rd, her attitude had changed. By showing her own card, she placed her Tutsi colleagues in danger, as Marie-Bernard recalled.

> Gertrude told us we must not show our identity cards at the road-blocks. But that was a lie, because she was the first to show her identity card. When we arrived at the military camp in Ngoma, we were stopped by soldiers at a road-block. Even before they asked us for them, Gertrude quickly showed her identity cards to betray us. We Tutsi nuns had left our identity cards at the monastery because carrying them would have made us even more readily identifiable. By some miracle, the soldiers let us pass and we reached the Parish of Ngoma.
> In the evening, Sr. Gertrude telephoned the military camp in Ngoma. I don't know whom she spoke to, but whoever it was, she was laughing and joking on the telephone.

Shortly after the nuns arrived at the parish, they received a visit from an interahamwe who told the priests assembled there that "they were looking for the Tutsi nuns." Régine described Sr. Gertrude's reaction.

> When Gertrude saw the interahamwe come in, she asked us if we had our identity cards. We thought that was strange, especially as prior to this, she had forbidden us from carrying them, saying that nuns were neither Hutu nor Tutsi, and that our sole identity was Christian. Now she was lecturing us as though we were abnormal to have left our identity cards behind. Sr. Domatile Uisitije said that it was she who had forbidden us from carrying our identity cards on the basis that we were all Christians.

On Sunday 24 April, Sr. Gertrude decided that the nuns should return to their monastery. They were accompanied by soldiers stationed at the nearby barracks of Camp Ngoma. They found the leading génocidaires of Sovu, including Rekeraho, waiting for them at the monastery when they reached there on Sunday evening, as Eugénie Mukagatera confirmed.

> We were driven back to Sovu by their soldiers. When they started taking us back to Sovu, I thought that our hour had arrived. When we got to the monastery, we saw the interahamwe waiting for us, including Rekeraho and Gaspard Rusanganwa, alias "Nyiramatwi."

Rekeraho said he was "surprised by their sudden departure" and telephoned Sr. Gertrude at Ngoma.

I asked her why they had left, but she was ashamed of what she had done the day before. I asked her to come back to Sovu and she agreed. They got back to the monastery under the escort of soldiers from Camp Ngoma. How and where did the nuns get to know these soldiers? I had never seen them together.

When the nuns left the monastery on the 23rd, and when they returned there on the 24th, they were accompanied and welcomed by Sovu's most feared génocidaires.

Destroying the Evidence

"Sr. Kizito, still with the jerrycans of petrol, was there with the killers who were checking if all the bodies were really dead."

Like a military commander surveying a battlefield after a victory, Sr. Kizito visited the massacre site shortly after the génocidaires had completed their "work." Adelice was lying among the dead bodies. She had been hit by three bullets and was severely injured. She saw Sr. Kizito as she wandered through the several thousand corpses at the health centre.

> My attention was caught by the well-known Sr. Julienne Kizito who had come to walk about all the bodies of the victims with a list in her hand. It was as if she was busy checking her list [to see] that all the refugees had been killed. The list she had was the one that had been drawn up at the time of the census on 19 April.
>
> She saw bank notes which had been torn up and said that this showed that the Tutsis were too cruel. I saw that she was really proud of the fact that all the refugees had been killed.

Séraphine, Adelice's sister, was also at the burnt-out site.

> There were a lot of women who were barely alive. But almost all the men were dead. I saw Sr. Kizito at the health centre. She moved all around the victims' bodies. She saw bank notes which the victims had torn before dying. She walked through all the rooms in the health centre where the corpses lay. She said it was the best way of killing them, seeing how bad the Tutsis were. She said all the Tutsis were very wicked because they had ripped up their notes before dying. She saw me. I heard and saw all that Kizito did.
>
> Kizito finally left. The génocidaires stayed behind, admiring the bravery of Kizito whom they described as their sister who was ready to help them finish off all the Tutsis by supplying petrol.

Josée Mukarwego could not accept that her seven children had perished at the health centre. She went to the garage in search of survivors. She did not find her children. Instead, she found Sr. Kizito and her allies. They were killing any survivors they could find.

> Sr. Kizito, still with the jerrycans of petrol, was there with the killers who were checking if all the bodies were really dead. Kizito was still distributing petrol. Next to her were Rekeraho and Byomboka. She could see very well that this petrol was being used to burn Tutsis and she continued to hand it out.

Although the fire at the garage the previous day had claimed many lives, there were still survivors inside and the militia were determined to kill them. Chantal Mukamisha survived the massacre at the health centre and had hidden among the dead and the wounded.

> I saw Sr. Kizito bringing over a jerry can, which can hold over seven bottles full of petrol. She gave them to Rushyana and Mucuceke and they threw it onto the garage, which they had previously not been able to enter.

But Chantal was also a target, and as she watched the militia burning the garage, she was hit by a bullet in the hip. Lying on the ground, she was presumed dead. As the militia continued to kill, Chantal managed to crawl into the bushes nearby. That night she made her way to the monastery where she thought she might find shelter, since she had once worked there and knew it well. She hid in the room where the tools were stored, but it was difficult to remain out of Kizito's reach.

> When Sr. Kizito saw me there, she called a policeman and told him that, as it was getting late, he should take me to the office of the commune the next day. The following morning she came back to see me in my hiding place, and recited the prayers, "Our Father" and "Hail Mary." Then she made the sign of the cross on my forehead and said: "The time has come for the soul to leave the body."

Fortunately, the policeman, who had been a family friend, agreed to spare Chantal.

While Sr. Kizito was checking her list to see who had died, the killers were executing the remaining refugees, all of them women and children. As in many of the other massacres during the 1994 genocide, the refugees begged to be shot with guns rather than hacked with machetes. Domatile Mukabanza had survived the massacre, along with her six children. She described how, as the militia looted from the refugees, her eldest daughter, Lucie Mugorewase, managed to escape. What happened to the other children is almost unbearable to even recount. The génocidaires killed the refugees as if they were on an assembly line. Five of Domatile's six children were murdered in front of her.

> They obliged us to line up in rows of 30 refugees. The lines were formed. I put my four children in front of me and my baby on my back. I told my children to pray since we were going to die soon. They made us go a little outside the health centre; they killed us just below the centre. They first took my five children. They were all killed in front of my eyes. Then they stuck a spear into my back which pierced the baby and wounded me seriously.
>
> The baby fell to the ground. He was already dead. They hit me a lot with the *massue* everywhere on the head. I fainted. Some minutes later, I felt something warm on my face. It was the blood which was flowing. I regained consciousness. I tried to open my eyes and I saw a certain Innocent Habyarimana who comes from my native hill of Nyanza. I tried to get up. He hit me on the head three times with a machete. This time, I felt I had been finished off. It was at about 10:00 a.m.

Though badly wounded, Domatile was still alive. There was another attempt to kill her.

> I heard them say: "This one is called Domatile." It seemed as if they were taking a census of the dead in order to tick their names against the list of the Tutsis who were to be killed. Then they threw me into a stream. Finally, they hit me with a weeding hoe on the head.

It rained during the night and Domatile awoke. She managed to get out of the river and collapsed under a tree. She then walked to Mbazi, to the homes of her Hutu mother's relatives. But her uncles and aunts threw her out. After hiding in a cemetery, a friend agreed to take her in and she eventually made her way to Ngoma.

As well as her involvement in the murders which took place at the health centre, there are allegations that Sr. Kizito took the victims' possessions to Huye commune office, to be shared out amongst the militia. Vénéranda Mukankusi had seen Sr. Kizito putting the refugees' possessions in a van. She went the monastery to try to retrieve her belongings. When she arrived, she met Sr. Kizito.

> I told Sr. Kizito, who knew me even before the genocide, that I had come to take my bags. This included clothes, beans, sorghum, cooking utensils etc... She was with a certain Gaspard, known as "Nyiramatwi." She told him to call Karekezi, a prominent killer, so that he could come and finish me off. She screamed insults against me, telling me to go away since I was an accomplice of the "snakes" [i.e. Tutsis]. That day, I saw the full extent of the cruelty of the nuns. [24]

Disposing of the Bodies

The militia worked together to bury the corpses as quickly and as efficiently as possible. The task began on 23 April, even while the surviving refugees were being grouped together to be finished off in one go. Initially, it was thought that the local peasants, who had helped to murder their neighbours, would offer to bury them without payment. But the genocide had, to a large extent, become a "business" and they were not prepared to oblige without payment, according to Rekeraho. Rekeraho said the militiamen turned to Gertrude to solve the problem.

---

[24] Interviewed in Sovu, 21 July 1995.

We suggested to Sr. Gertrude that she ask the nuns' relatives to pay 100,000 francs so that we could finish burying their brothers.

But according to the nuns who had relatives at the monastery, Sr. Gertrude paid the money herself. Rekeraho continued his account.

Gertrude gave the money to me in person. I, in turn gave it to Kamanayo and Rushyana, in the presence of councillor Muvunyi and Gaspard Rusanganwa.

There were too many bodies to count, but there were definitely thousands of them. I couldn't give an exact figure. We were no longer normal. We buried the people. Then we tried to recover the equipment of the health centre that had been looted by the militia. The centre could no longer operate, so Gaspard Rusanganwa's wife, a nurse, began treating people in a tent donated by the Red Cross.

Rekeraho mobilised the work force and supervised them while he chatted with Gertrude and Kizito. He fetched Muvunyi, the councillor of Sovu, from his house. Muvunyi gave additional details about the burial.

When we arrived at the monastery, they were burying the Tutsis' bodies. I helped with the burial while Rekeraho had a chat with Sr. Kizito and Sr. Gertrude. I buried Cassien Karido; his wife, Nyirarudadari; his mother; old Damascène Kamuyango; his wife, Mukarubuga; Jean Nyamaswa and his wife; old Phillipe; Habiyakare and many others. There were perhaps over 4,000 corpses.

To expedite the task, the men were divided into groups.

There were three teams; one at the monastery and health centre, one in the bush and another at the cross-roads near Matabaro's house. Rekeraho came to supervise the burials, along with some other officers who arrived in two jeeps at about 11.00 a.m.

Muvunyi said that the officers joined Rekeraho in shooting those refugees who were still alive, while he and the other men disposed of the bodies in the fields neighbouring the monastery. He said Rekeraho was going back and forth between the monastery and the burial teams. Muvunyi accompanied him during a visit to the monastery.

He was driving the nuns' ambulance and he asked me to follow him. He had blood on his multi-coloured shirt and khaki trousers. He asked for water to wash and Sr. Kizito brought him some. She also brought him a jug of milk and he drank three mugs. Rusanganwa and I drank some beer.

Sr. Kizito was very happy, according to Muvunyi.

While we were drinking milk and beer with Kizito, Rekeraho kept complimenting her on her courage. He told her: "If I could, I'd appoint you Mother Superior of this monastery." She roared with laughter and was obviously very pleased. Gaspard and I left Kizito and Rekeraho alone in the foyer after that, as they seemed to have a lot to say to each other.

It was clear that the militia were trying to dispose of the bodies quickly. Domatile, who was just regaining consciousness, overheard them complaining.

Around 1:00 p.m., I was able to hear again. I heard the voices of certain génocidaires like Warrant Officer Rekeraho and Gaspard, alias "Nyiramatwi." They were saying: "Bury quickly because at 2:00 p.m., we are going to finish the Tutsis who are at the commune office of Huye." They gathered the bodies of the victims and buried them on Karido's land, which was next door.

But there were so many dead, that the burial took place over several days. Once finished, Rekeraho and his men lost no time in resuming the genocide. This time however, it was Sr. Kizito and Sr. Gertrude themselves who took the lead in singling out the victims.

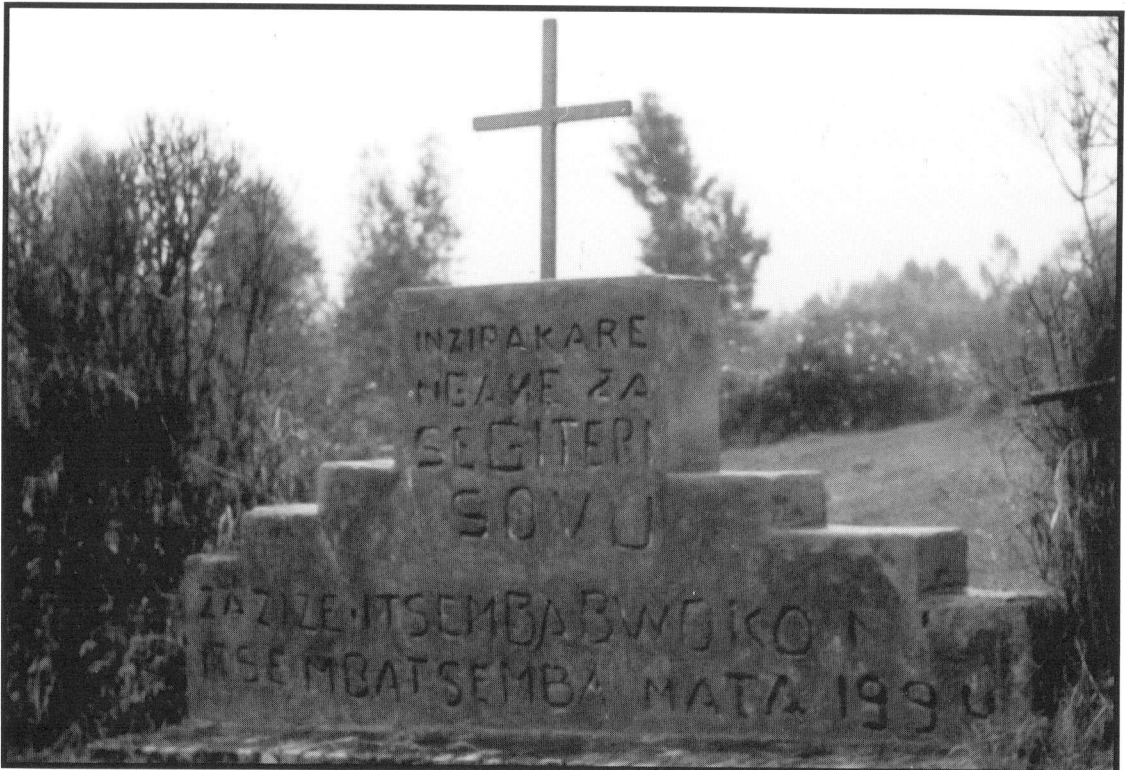

Masse graves near the monastery in Sovu

The Killings at the Monastery
25 April 1994

"Sr. Gertrude and Sr. Kizito forced out the remaining Tutsis"

Despite the best efforts of Sr. Gertrude, a number of Tutsis had managed to stay inside the monastery and escape the massacre at the health centre. Among them were the relatives of some of the nuns; Tutsis who had come to Sovu for a training course and workers of the monastery.[25] There were also some survivors of the massacre of 22 April. Several of the nuns have spoken of the events of 25 April, when Emmanuel Rekeraho came to the monastery, with other leading génocidaires, to kill the refugees. The militiamen forced the majority of them out of the building and then killed them near the monastery. But Rekeraho decided that he would exempt the nuns' relatives from the slaughter, a decision which, the nuns say, Sr. Gertrude made plain she did not agree with. The nuns' accounts of what happened suggest that not only did the Mother Superior and Sr. Kizito support Rekeraho's aims in killing the refugees at the monastery, but they believed he did not go far enough.

As Rekeraho has admitted, he and the other organisers of the genocide in Sovu did not consider the massacre of the Tutsis at the health centre and at the garage sufficient. With the burial out of the way, on Monday 25 April they went in search of the Tutsis who remained alive in Sovu. Their first destination was the Benedictine monastery; Rekeraho explained why.

> We were in a hurry to go and kill the Tutsis in the monastery as well since Sr. Gertrude had not concealed the fact from anyone that there were Tutsis there. Everyone was talking about it.

Rekeraho visited the monastery on the 24th, and Marie-Bernard Kayitesi saw him. She said:

> Rekeraho wanted to kill all the wounded refugees who were at the monastery. He left, saying he would be back the next day. That evening, Gertrude told all the Sisters whose relatives had taken refuge in the monastery to send them away in order to save the monastery. We turned a deaf ear to her request.

Marie-Bernard Kayitesi spoke of the "desperate people, the wounded survivors who, on the evening of 22 April, broke into the monastery and occupied the monastery's guest quarters by force." Rekeraho gave a detailed account of how most of them met their death, and of the actions of Sr. Gertrude and Sr. Kizito.

> We set off; Jean-Baptiste Muvunyi, Gaspard and I, along with the soldiers, gendarmes and a lot of militiamen. When we reached the main gate, I asked the policeman who was guarding the nuns to fetch the Mother Superior and Sr. Julienne Kizito for me. The two nuns came out at once, together with another nun from Kibungo whose name I don't know. I told the nuns that we had finished killing the *Inyenzi* at the health centre, and that we wanted to kill the ones in the monastery.

Sr. Gertrude did not oppose Rekeraho; rather she assisted him.

> Sr. Gertrude told us that there were indeed a lot of them hiding in the monastery. The nuns then opened the main gate for us, as there was a padlock on it. The three of us went in, leaving the soldiers and gendarmes outside. Gertrude then called all the nuns into a large room, perhaps the hall used for meetings. I then said that we had decided to finish off all the Tutsis. There were more than 20 or 30 nuns there. I asked Kizito to draw me up a list of all the Tutsis there, and of all the Tutsi nuns' relatives.

Gertrude and Kizito themselves took the initiative to force the Tutsis out of their hiding places.

---

[25] About twenty workers were killed together with their families. They included Anastase Nkurunziza; Cyrille Ndanga; Augustin Mpambara; Antoine Ntezimana; Jean Sebuhinyori, the father of Régine Niyonsaba; Emmanuel Ntezimana; Jean Ruhinguka; Boniface Karabaranga; Chantal Mukashyaka and Claire Umulisa.

We did not search their rooms. Gertrude and Kizito went off themselves and made all the Tutsis come out of hiding. They got 20 people out straight away. Gaspard told them there must be more. That was when I asked for a list, and said I wanted all the Tutsis to come out, except for the nuns' relatives. I checked against the list that I had in my hand. Sr. Kizito brought some milk and offered my companions some beer. I was hungry, and that was why I didn't want to drink any alcohol.

Marie-Bernard highlighted Sr. Gertrude's efforts to hasten the refugees' death.

On 25 April, Gertrude, Rekeraho and Rusanganwa had a private meeting. After the meeting, Gertrude went to see the refugees in the guest quarters and told them: "Peace has been restored. Now you can go back to your own hills and your neighbours will help you to repair your homes. Those of you who are not natives of Sovu will be given passes so you will have no difficulty in getting home." It was a ruse to get them to leave the monastery. The refugees, who had no other choice, obeyed her and left all the quarters they were occupying.

Augustin Ngirinshuti witnessed the fate of two employees of the monastery.

Kizito came in with a ladder, not far from my hiding place, and forced out two Tutsi workers, including Sister Bernadette's father. They begged for mercy but she refused their pleas, and handed them over to the militia who killed them.

Régine Niyonsaba, whose mother and younger sisters were at the monastery, knew what Rekeraho's arrival would mean.

At about 9:00 a.m., on Monday 25 April, Sr. Gertrude called us together, along with our families and survivors from the health centre. We assembled in the big foyer in the presence of Warrant Officer Rekeraho. Gertrude then addressed us, saying that the Tutsis must leave the monastery and go home, as they were putting its security at risk. I don't remember if Rekeraho said anything. But I know that just the sight of Rekeraho made the Tutsis who were there realise that their last moments were drawing near. The Tutsis then began leaving the monastery. They went and hid behind the wall. We accompanied them to see where they were going.

Sr. Bernadette Nyirandamutsa asked Rekeraho to spare the nuns' close relatives. Rekeraho agreed, adding "anyway, most of them are women and old men who won't be running the country." Marie-Bernard's two brothers were included in this reprieve.

Rekeraho gathered all the Tutsi nuns whose relatives were taking refuge at the monastery around him. He told us: "I can see that your relatives add up to fewer than thirty people and most of them are old men, old women and small children. They are not likely to be a problem to us. I, Rekeraho, am satisfied and I shall not be coming back to kill any more Tutsis here. Now, you can hide your relatives wherever you like-up in the ceiling or wherever. Your monastery is huge. I'm sure nobody will come to bother you and I shall make frequent visits to make sure you are safe and to let you know what is happening." Then he left. He was right; our relatives totalled between 20-30 people.
    Rekeraho was the head of the militia in the region and so had the power of life or death. So we believed him.

Annonciata Mukagasana listened with the other nuns as Rekeraho made his promise.

Rekeraho came and calmed us, calling us his girls. He said no one would touch us unless the RPF entered Butare. He even reassured the Tutsi Sisters' relatives; now there were only women and one old man left, as the men and young people had been massacred. Rekeraho was accompanied by Gaspard Rusanganwa and the councillor, Jean-Baptiste Muvunyi.

The nuns' families returned to the monastery. But the other candidates for death were not so fortunate, as Rekeraho explained.

Gertrude and Kizito forced out the remaining Tutsis. We took them and handed them over to the soldiers, gendarmes and peasants who had been waiting for them impatiently. They began the carnage. It was exactly like what happened at the health centre except they weren't burnt alive with petrol.

Before he "handed them over," Rekeraho picked out the people he wanted to be killed.

I grouped the Tutsis into three groups: workers, other refugees and the families of the nuns. I asked the latter to go back to the monastery and told the others to get out so that they could be massacred by the militia and the soldiers. But of course I didn't do anything without first talking it over with Kizito and Gertrude.

Marie-Bernard witnessed Rekeraho's selection process.

Once they were out in the interior courtyard of the monastery, Rekeraho divided them into three groups to make them more readily identifiable. "Those of you who are from Sovu, stand over there," he said. "Those of you who are from other communes and hills, stand over here, and the relatives of Tutsi nuns, stand over there." He ordered the first two groups to leave the monastery. Once they were outside the gates, he gave a whistle, and the militiamen who were waiting for them rushed upon the refugees and killed them all. There were about 100 refugees, including Tutsi visitors who were at the monastery for a training course funded by the Americans.

Annonciata said that from inside the monastery they could hear the gunfire and grenades which signalled the deaths of the refugees.

The Tutsi staff of the monastery and the survivors of the health centre left. They were taken into the bush behind the monastery by Rekeraho and other militiamen. A few minutes later, there was an uproar—groaning, gunfire and the explosion of grenades. After the killings, they came into the monastery to get some hoes, to dig mass graves.

With Rekeraho gone, Sr. Gertrude is said to have sent one of the nuns' relatives, a young girl, to their death.

I saw Sr. Gertrude throw out the cousin of Sr. Théonila[26], a girl from Maraba, just when Rekeraho and his militia were executing the others in the bush behind the monastery. The girl begged Sister Gertrude saying: "Save me, woman of God." She answered, "Go and join your family." And the poor little girl went to join those who were being killed in the bush.

Sr. Théonila tried to reason with Gertrude, but to no avail. Another of the nuns recalled their exchange.

Gertrude threw out the cousin of Sr. Théonila. She was a girl of 16 who had been cut on the head with a machete. Her case was very moving. Still, Gertrude didn't want this girl to stay in the monastery and she told Sr. Théonila to expel her. Sr. Théonila, incapable of doing so, begged Sr. Gertrude to let her stay the monastery, at the same time explaining to her the danger that she was in. Gertrude refused and she forced the wounded girl to leave the monastery to go and to die with the others.

There followed a brief lull, during which the nuns' relatives awaited their fate, in a state of "controlled panic" in the words of one nun. Sr. Gertrude's attitude and actions left them in no doubt that their days were numbered.

---

[26] Sr. Théonila was killed in Gikongoro in July 1994.

A Sentence of Death
6 May 1994

"Sister Kizito showed them the bedrooms where our relatives were hiding."

As the days went by, it became increasingly clear that Sr. Gertrude and Sr. Kizito were determined to deliver the relatives of the Tutsi nuns hiding at the monastery to their death, even if this meant flouting Rekeraho's instructions. Saying she feared an attack upon the monastery by the militia, the Mother Superior repeatedly told the nuns to make their relatives leave. But having no alternative, the nuns refused and lived in fear of another massacre.

The nuns who had relatives hiding in the monastery were Sr. Bénédicte Kagaju; Sr. Bernadette Nyirandamutsa; Sr. Marie-Bernard Kayitesi; Sr. Fortunata Mukagasana; Sr. Scholastique Mukangira; Sr. Thérèse Mukarubibi; a number of novices, including Régine Niyonsaba and some of the applicants. They had brought them into the monastery discreetly without informing the Mother Superior. They occupied the cellar, bedrooms, ceilings and the hostelry. Marie-Bernard Kayitesi, whose two brothers were amongst the refugees, spoke of the relentless pressure from Sr. Gertrude.

> Two days after Rekeraho's departure, Sr. Gertrude began to threaten us again. She would not leave us in peace. Every morning she came knocking at the doors of those of us who had relatives at the monastery, saying: "Rekeraho told you lies. Rekeraho told you lies. He's just looking for reasons to come and destroy our monastery by labelling me an RPF accomplice. This is why I am begging you to remove your relatives. Please, they must leave the monastery." Once again, we turned a deaf ear to her requests.
>
> Every time she repeated her threats, we stood our ground and said to her: "You must understand, once and for all, that none of us are going to do what you want us to do." Every time the bourgmestre came to the monastery, she pleaded with him to drive our relatives out of the monastery. But he told her they had to await Rekeraho's decision, for he would wreak havoc if his orders were not obeyed.

Gertrude argued that the refugees were accomplices of the RPF and that their presence endangered the security of the monastery. Still, the nuns refused to betray their families. To Annonciata Mukagasana, a young woman just beginning her life as a nun, Gertrude's behaviour was incomprehensible.

> Gertrude even asked the Sisters to remove their relations. She kept saying the Sisters must comply, or the monastery would be destroyed by the interahamwe. It was shocking. Régine, Fortunata, Bernadette and Marie-Bernard had relations in the monastery. There were Sr. Bénédicte's niece, Aline; Sr. Thérèse's younger sister; Sr. Fortunata's relatives, including her elderly father, Cyrille, and Régine's mother and two younger sisters. They thought they would not die there because there weren't any men and boys, and Rekeraho had given them his promise.

On the morning of 23 April, Gertrude made yet another appeal to her fellow-nuns, as Annonciata recalled.

> Gertrude said very loudly in the chapel that she did not start the war, and that all the Sisters should get their relatives out of the monastery, or the killers would come and attack the monastery.

The nuns whose parents, brothers and sisters had come to them for protection could not consider forcing them to leave; they knew that they would have no chance of survival outside. Moreover Rekeraho, the commander of the génocidaires in Sovu, had personally assured them that he would not kill them at the monastery. When her entreaties failed to move the nuns, Gertrude changed tactics, telling the nuns that she didn't have any food, and that they should contribute money. The nuns did so, but, as Régine pointed out, she was clearly not satisfied.

We were still in a state of panic. Gertrude came and asked our families to make a contribution to the cost of food. Everyone gave what they had. But it was clear that Gertrude was becoming increasingly agitated. She insisted that we ask our families to leave. We explained to her that it was impossible to let our relatives go to their deaths, as long as we could still hide them. She then suggested that we go and hide them somewhere else, a long way from the monastery. We refused to do so.

On 5 May, the Mother Superior sent a letter to the bourgmestre of Huye commune, Jonathan Ruremesha. According to Marie-Bernard, "she gave the letter to Sr. Kizito to deliver by hand to the bourgmestre." The original of the letter was found in Butare after the genocide. African Rights has obtained a copy of this letter. In it the Mother Superior makes no mention of the massacres which had taken place at the health centre, nor of the terror which caused people to seek sanctuary at the monastery. The callous attitude of Sr. Gertrude towards people whose lives were in immediate danger is made plain. She wrote:

> In the last weeks, there has been, in the monastery of Sovu, the usual arrival of visitors. Normally, their stay does not extend beyond a week. Some were on a mission and others on holiday or on a prayer retreat.
>
> With the resumption of the war throughout the territory of the country, other individuals have come unexpectedly and do not want to leave our monastery, even though we have no way of feeding them... It is a long time since I asked the administration of the commune to come and order all these people to return to their homes or to go elsewhere because we cannot keep them in our monastery.
>
> I am pleading with you, Mr bourgmestre, to come and help us settle this problem, at the latest on 6 May 1994 so that the monastery can take up its daily activities without any anxiety.[27]

The letter was copied to the préfet and the military commander, two men who had done much to advance the genocide in Butare. Marie-Bernard described Gertrude's mood after the letter was despatched.

> Sr. Gertrude did not sleep at all on the night of 5 May. She did not give us a moment's peace. She came knocking at our doors, telling us again and again that we must make our relatives go away. We told her to leave everyone alone and trust in the will of God rather than sullying her soul unnecessarily.
>
> Gertrude said to me: "If you don't get them out of the monastery, I know just what I'm going to do. And anyway, what were they running away from? What were they up to, coming here?" She said it as though she had no idea what was going on.

On the morning of 6 May, Marie-Bernard listened as Gertrude delivered her final ultimatum; clearly she was expecting the militia to arrive but was disappointed.

> Very early on the morning of 6 May, just after morning prayer, Sr. Gertrude addressed us all: "Before almighty God, I beg the Sisters who have relatives in the monastery to remove them, unconditionally. We cannot risk our lives for them. If you don't remove them of your own free will, then the State will use its powers to remove them."
>
> At about 8:00 a.m., she realised that she had not been obeyed and drove off in the monastery's car. This time, she took the Volkswagen and drove off with Gaspard Rusanganwa, who lived not far from the monastery. At about noon, Gertrude came back, more furious than ever.

She had, nevertheless, accomplished her mission.

> We were about to sit down to lunch when the militia surrounded the monastery. We could see they were waiting for something. At about 3:00 p.m., the bourgmestre, Jonathan Ruremesha, arrived in his car with two policemen armed with guns. Gaspard Rusanganwa arrived immediately afterwards. What a coincidence! They addressed all the nuns, but the militia stayed outside.

---

[27] Translation of the letter written in Kinyarwanda by Sr. Gertrude.

Another nun confirmed Marie-Bernard's account.

On the morning of 6 May, in church after the prayers of Laudes, while still kneeling, Gertrude said in a loud voice: "Before God Almighty, I am asking all the Sisters who have relatives here to expel them, otherwise we will use force."

She left in the Volkswagen with Gaspard Rusanganwa, alias "Nyiramatwi." No one knew where she had gone. At about 3:00 p.m., the interahamwe surrounded the monastery. After a moment, there was bourgmestre Ruremesha's car parked outside with some policemen. We saw the arrival of Rusanganwa and Gertrude who had gone to call them. They made all the refugees leave. The policemen forced them out and robbed them.

The refugees from Sovu and Maraba were forced to return to their homes. The interahamwe killed them once they had left the monastery. Others were shot by the policeman, Xavier, who was guarding the place. Ruremesha drove those who had come from other places away in his van. We don't know where they were killed.

According to Marie-Bernard, the bourgmestre, Jonathan Ruremesha, gave Sr. Gertrude the opportunity to save some of the refugees.

The bourgmestre spoke, saying: "There is nothing more we can do. Your relatives are going to die. But this young girl for example—referring to the younger sister of Sr. Thérèse—if Sr. Gertrude is willing to give her a veil and disguise her as a novice, she may live." Gertrude categorically refused, saying; "No, no, they must all leave."

Sr. Kizito showed the policemen the rooms occupied by the refugees.

Kizito led the way and the communal policemen followed her. She showed them all the rooms in which the refugees were staying. They made them all come down and stand in front of the bourgmestre. He used the very same procedure that Rekeraho had used, putting natives of Sovu on one side and people from elsewhere on the other. He said he was going to help them to go home. Sr. Bernadette's father, who was not from Huye, asked the bourgmestre how he was going to get through the murderers' road-blocks. The bourgmestre gave him a little hand-written note, but that was just to get rid of him.

For Marie-Bernard, it was the last time she saw her two brothers.

Ruremesha told some of the refugees to get into his car and drove them to the commune office. His passengers included my two brothers: Placide Seti, 20, single, who had come from Kigali; and Déo Gatete, 23, married and father of two children, who had come from Gikongoro. Chantal, the wife of Charles Butera, was also one of his passengers. We still don't know where they were killed. Other refugees were killed as they left the monastery, including Sr. Fortunata's father, Cyrille Ndanga.

As a last gesture of love, some of the nuns paid to have their relatives shot. Marie-Bernard continued her account.

Some of the nuns gave money to Xavier, the policeman who was supposed to be guarding the monastery, so that their relatives might be shot rather than hacked to death by machete. They paid 7,000 francs per person.

"Some of the nuns told Gertrude they were going to follow the militia so that they could die with their relatives. Gertrude asked them what they were waiting for. After the slaughter, Sr. Gertrude was satisfied."

She locked the entrance to the monastery and kept the keys. There was a deathly silence amongst us. We each kept our own counsel. It was terrible. Sr. Véronique, an American, saw all of this and was as upset as we were.

Régine's mother and two younger sisters had been hiding at the monastery. She also said Sr. Gertrude had told the nuns to force their relatives to leave and that she went out in the car with the assistant bourgmestre, Gaspard Rusanganwa. Régine described the evident agitation of Sr. Kizito, then the part she played in finding the victims.

> She couldn't stay still and wouldn't speak to us. She asked the workmen whom she was in charge of that day to cut down all the grass around the monastery, to reveal any enemies hiding there. When Gertrude came back in the afternoon, she saw the workmen cutting down the grass, but did nothing to stop them.
>
> At about 3:00 p.m. we heard whistles and tambourines as we had done on 22 April when they killed people at the health centre. We quickly realised that this time it was our turn. We could see them advancing on us in the hostelry. There was a gate between the monastery and Gaspard's house. I saw Gertrude head for this gate; some time later, she came back with Gaspard.
>
> Ruremesha, the bourgmestre of Huye, arrived with two policemen. He and Kizito forced our relatives out of the hostelry. Kizito showed them the bedrooms where our relatives were hiding. First they were lined up outside the main entrance; then the bourgmestre asked them to go home. If they were too frightened to do so, he said he would take them to the office of the préfecture. He made a very long speech. Some of them got in a van; I don't know where they went.

Régine's mother was shot in front of her.

> Mother and Fortunata's two younger sisters were afraid to get in the van, and walked around the monastery, heading for the banana grove. Fortunata and I followed them. We asked the policeman to kill us together with our relatives. He replied that he had not received permission to kill nuns. Mother and Fortunata's sisters begged him to kill them, so that they would be spared the torture of the interahamwe.

The only way to avoid a machete was to pay to be shot.

> The policeman then asked for money. One of Fortunata's sisters paid him. He then shot them. I saw them die. They immediately ordered us back to the monastery, because he was going to call the militia to make sure that he really had killed them.
>
> When we reached the monastery, only the nuns were there. I collapsed and had difficulty breathing. I left Sr. Fortunata because I wanted to be alone. I was suffering from high blood pressure. Sr. Solange and Sr. Scholastique came to see me.

Kizito took personal charge of searching the ceiling; Annonciata witnessed the precautions she took.

> There was a man who used to help Kizito use the ladder to search for Tutsis who had hidden in the ceiling. She managed to get a lot of them out; I myself saw two youngsters she got down from the ceiling.

Augustin Ngirinshuti also spoke of the arrival of the bourgmestre at the monastery and the events which followed.

> The bourgmestre of Huye arrived with two vehicles, one of them a Hilux, to take away some of the Tutsi nuns' relatives and to kill the rest not far from the monastery. When he arrived with some policemen, he asked Sr. Gertrude to bring out all those Tutsis who were still there. She did so herself. The bourgmestre then asked for them to be divided into groups, according to their préfectures. They told him I was from Gisenyi and he asked them to leave me there until Monday. He made some of them get into his vehicle. Regarding the ones from Sovu, including the relatives of Bernadette, Régine and Fortunata, he told the policemen to "accompany" them. They shot them a few minutes later; I heard the shots.

Augustin's wife Marcelline managed to hide in the ceiling while the other Tutsis were killed.

While others were being killed, I was in the ceiling, but I heard the shots which killed the nuns' relatives. The bourgmestre came and took away the survivors, including Régine's mother and her two younger sisters; Fortunata's father and the others. They left me alone because my husband was a Hutu.

The councillor, Jean-Baptiste Muvunyi, saw the refugees as they were led to their deaths.

On 6 May, Rusanganwa organised communal labour (*umuganda*) so that people could build a rural dispensary, because the other one had become contaminated. That day, I saw the bourgmestre, Rekeraho, Sr. Kizito and Sr. Gertrude force people out of hiding in the monastery. They were relatives of the Tutsi nuns at the monastery.

One of the nuns had hidden her father and her younger married sister in a corner of the monastery. Her father was killed, but the sister, Caritas, cited above, survived. Caritas described their ordeal.

There must have been around 60 of us there. Sr. Kizito put increasing pressure on her colleagues, threatening those who were hiding their people in the monastery. All the refugees at the health centre had been assassinated. But this did not deter Gertrude from continuing to chase us out of the monastery. Such was her malice that she went, once more, to fetch the bourgmestre, Jonathan Ruremesha, from Huye to come and force us to leave. Sisters Bernadette, Marie-Bernard, Scholastique, Régine, and many others pleaded on our behalf. But despite their pleas we were finally thrown out of the monastery.

"How Sister Gertrude could show no mercy, faced with children who had their arms extended out to her—begging her to hide them—I don't know. Instead, she told them to go and die with their parents."

The bourgmestre told every refugee to return to the commune they came from. Those who did not come from Huye were herded on to buses, believing they would be returned to their homes. But they were all murdered on the Butare to Gikongoro road.

Despite the danger, elderly refugees found it difficult to overcome the habit of a lifetime—obedience and confidence in authority.

My father had not understood that throwing us out of the monastery was tantamount to handing us over to our killers. He went to the bourgmestre and asked for papers or some form of authorisation to allow us to pass through the road blocks, as we wanted to return to our commune. The bourgmestre asked him to draw up a list of all those who had left this commune, but there were only myself, my brother, my younger sister and my father. Without any further ado, the bourgmestre signed the list and gave it back to my father. We set off.

The refugees had feared certain death if they were expelled from the monastery. They had hardly left the monastery when this came true for Caritas' family.

When we reached the bottom of the hill and met up with the Butare-Gikongoro road, we were stopped by the interahamwe at a road block. There, both my father and brother were murdered.

Caritas was spared, but only to be raped by the militia.

One of the militiaman at the road block knocked me to the ground with a blow from his club. The militia then stripped me completely naked. One of them took me for his wife.

ABA BAGUYE MURI MONASTERE ISOVU LE 6/5/94

• Madame Therese Mukabutera 1948-1994
  Secteur Sovu / Commune Huye
• ABANA BE BABIRI Marie Reine Mukabutera 1989-1994
                 Marcella Uwampaye Maria 1991-1994

• Odetta Nyirahabimana ——— 1964-1994
  Secteur Sovu / Commune Huye
• UMWANA WE Jean Berchmas Rugema 1993-1994

• Athanasie Mukakayumba 1966-1994
  Secteur Sovu / Commune Huye
       (Murumuna wa Odetta)

Monuments dedicated to the victims

After a few days, Caritas asked this militiaman to accompany her to her sector to collect her personal belongings. When she arrived home, she was welcomed back by her husband, but only to learn that her mother and younger sister had died at the Parish of Rugango.

Rekeraho, who described himself as a "criminal" and a "coward", explained why he wanted to spare the nuns' relatives.

I killed and I made people kill. Even though I killed so many people, frankly I took pity on those poor women and old people. Also, my old primary school teacher was among the nuns' relatives. In addition, the nuns had contributed to progress in the region.

He spoke of Gertrude's letter to Ruremesha.

I have seen with my own eyes a letter which Sr. Gertrude sent to bourgmestre Jonathan Ruremesha asking him to come and evacuate the Tutsis from the monastery. Where did Gertrude want the nun's relatives to be taken, since she knew very well that they could be killed anywhere? No, Gertrude and Kizito don't deserve to be called nuns. They have never served God.

Rekeraho finished his explanation with this telling insight into the mindset of the génocidaires.

When I realised the extent of the killings, I quickly understood that this could not remain hidden for ever. I realised that sooner or later this would become known, but also that we would not enjoy impunity forever. I knew that nuns were part of the elite of the country. I told myself that one day they were going to testify. Of course I wanted them to speak well of me. This is why, even if I killed others, I wanted to spare at least their families.

A Commitment to Genocide

"They shared our hatred for the Tutsis"

There is clear evidence that Sr. Gertrude and Sr. Kizito cooperated with militiamen throughout the genocide and assisted them in carrying out the massacres which took place at Sovu in April and May 1994. The survivors and witnesses whose testimonies have been included in this report emphasise the nuns' alliance with Emmanuel Rekeraho and Gaspard Rusanganwa, two of the most prominent génocidaires in Sovu, as key to their direct part in the violence.

Sr. Kizito in particular became virtually inseparable from Rekeraho, as her older brother, Tharcisse Ngoboka, 45, testifies. He comes from cellule Kigarama in Sovu. He was a watchman in 1994 and was unemployed at the time of the interview.

> I saw Rekeraho on more than one occasion with my younger sister, Julienne Mukabutera. There wasn't a day when I didn't see them in town together. Even people from Sovu had told me that Rekeraho was with my sister all the time, accompanied by Sr. Gertrude.
>
> Rekeraho was an evil man who hated Tutsis. My sister and he were hardly ever apart during the genocide. They were always together in the beige-coloured ambulance, or at the monastery. They had become almost like man and wife. They had not been so close before Habyarimana's death. Even if my younger sister did not kill anyone, she was certainly aware of everything Rekeraho was doing. He acted like a real leader and used to tour all the sectors, and even the nearby communes, organising the interahamwe.

Despite her relations with Rekeraho, Kizito did not use her influence to protect Tharcisse's Tutsi wife.

> What I find it disturbing is that while my wife, a Tutsi, Valéria Mukabahizi, was in danger and had to hide at my father's house, my sister, Kizito, never once came to see her. She can't tell me she had no time to do so, nor that she was scared. I can't help thinking that she had joined Rekeraho's side. If she really did kill people or had them killed, it is up to her alone to face the consequences of her actions.[28]

Marcelline also noted that Kizito was frequently in the company of the interahamwe.

> Kizito accompanied the militia on their continuous dawn searches for Tutsis, both in the bush and in the ceilings. I saw Kizito with Rekeraho and the interahamwe all the time.[29]

The nuns and novices who were in Sovu at the time have not forgotten Rekeraho's frequent visits to the monastery. Eugenie Mukagatera, a novice, said Rekeraho would hold "secret meetings with Kizito and Gertrude."

According to a fellow nun, Kizito barely spent any time at the monastery during April-June.

> Apart from Kizito and Gertrude, the other Sisters did not go out. Kizito used to go out during the night; everybody used to wonder where she was going.

Annonciata made a similar observation.

> Kizito was hardly ever at the monastery; she was out all the time.

Marie-Bernard Kayitesi commented on the reasons for Kizito's absence.

> From the beginning of the crisis, Sr. Kizito showed her face at the community only very occasionally. She spent all her time up on Sovu hill, talking to the militia. Kizito was very friendly with the

---

[28] Interviewed in Sovu, 10 May 1999.
[29] Interviewed in Ruhashya, 2 June 1999.

murderers, who treated her like a sister. Kizito was a native of Sovu, so she knew the region well and was very familiar with the surrounding area. She told us all of this before 22 April.

Jean-Baptiste Muvunyi, the councillor of Sovu, was aware of the ties between Rekeraho and the two nuns.

On the evening of 21 April, just before 8.00 p.m. Rekeraho came to see me. He tapped on the window and asked me to go to the monastery with him. I told him I couldn't do so given the hour. Besides, I didn't know what he intended to do at the monastery at such a time, but I knew he was a frequent visitor there.

Lambert Nsabimana said that when he chatted to some interahamwe, they praised "the virility" (*ubugabo*) of Sr. Gertrude and Sr. Kizito. Lambert said that he was "not surprised by what they said." He explained the reasons.

On Monday 18 April, the bourgmestre, Jonathan Ruremesha, arrived at the monastery with some soldiers and asked only for Kizito and Gertrude, even though there were about twenty nuns there. They had a long conversations, but I don't know what about.
They were always going out, especially Kizito. On Thursday, 21 April, when I went and asked for a mattress and a blanket, she was in a hurry, and said that she was going to the commune for an emergency meeting.

Claver Rugwizintare caught sight of Kizito and Rekeraho together, in the monastery's vehicle. Claver, 71, is a native of cellule Kigarama. He is detained in Karubanda Prison in Butare in connection with the genocide.

One day I saw Rekeraho with Sr. Kizito in a beige-coloured ambulance from the health centre. They passed me at the turn to Nyanza [in Huye]. I had just withdrawn my April pension money at the office of the préfecture.[30]

One of the men Rekeraho drove in the ambulance is Innocent Ngirunigize, alias "Hérode" from Kigarama. Innocent, 30, used to be a watchman and is currently imprisoned in Karubanda Prison. He admits killing a lot of people in Huye and says that Rekeraho led him and other militiamen when they went out to kill Tutsis.

One night, at about 7:00 p.m., I killed Bertin at Migabo's house. My employer, Munyeshyaka, had asked me to go instead of him as he was unwell. He got me a spear and a machete. Rekeraho drove me in the nuns' ambulance and we went to the monastery with him to make the Tutsis who were hiding there leave. I saw Sr. Kizito talking to Rekeraho upstairs.[31]

Lucie Mugorewase, a young peasant who lived in Kigarama, mentioned other génocidaires in Sovu who regarded Kizito as "one of them."

Gertrude and Kizito collaborated with some of the leading génocidaires in Huye like Pierre Rushyana and his sons; Jean Maniraho; Etienne Rugombyumugabo and Théoneste Kagina. When the interahamwe came, they initially addressed Kizito. They called her their representative, saying that she was a real "Sister" who would not tolerate *Inyenzi* in her monastery.[32]

According to many people who were in Sovu at the time, even the killers were surprised by the uncompromising attitudes of Sr. Kizito and Sr. Gertrude. After the killings of 6 May, Sr. Gertrude

---

[30] Interviewed in Ngoma, 11 May 1999.
[31] Interviewed in Ngoma, 13 May 1999.
[32] Interviewed in Sovu, 22 July 1995.

asked Marcelline Nyirakimonyo and her husband, Augustin Ngirinshuti, to leave the monastery. Augustin and his wife failed to understand her reasoning.

> Gertrude came to see us at about 3:00 a.m. one night and told us to leave. We begged to stay, but she refused. My wife is a Tutsi; she told me to leave with her and the others. Fortunately for us, the policeman, Xavier, made her see reason, asking her where she intended to take us so late at night.

Marcelline feared for her life.

> Gertrude came to see us at 3:00 a.m. one night and told us to leave our hiding place and go outside, when there were militiamen out there. My husband did not want to leave. I reacted angrily and told Sr. Gertrude that "leaving the house is the same as leaving Rwanda." Even the policeman who was with there asked where she intended to take us at that late hour. She said that if that was the way he saw things, we could go back inside, and we did so.

Saying that "Kizito was nastier than the interahamwe," Alice Mukankundiye underlined the intensity of Sr. Kizito's hatred of Tutsis. Again, the policeman, Xavier Nsanzabera, who had himself shot into the refugees on 22 April, had to intervene. Alice described the scene.

> One day, a Tutsi woman who was mentally disturbed came into the monastery. The interahamwe refused to kill her, saying that their beliefs wouldn't allow it[33] and that she was a symbol of the Tutsis as a whole.
>   When Kizito saw the woman, she told the communal policeman called Xavier, who was guarding the monastery, to shoot her. But the policeman refused, pointing out that the woman was mentally deranged.

The disturbed woman, Hélène Mukandori, had a son with Xavier's nephew, Innocent Rubunda.

> Kizito replied that she was not mad, and that it was a ploy dreamed up by the Tutsis to act as if they were all lunatics in order not to get shot. Her persistent demand that Xavier shoot the woman required him to explain that he had known the woman even before the genocide, and that she had been mad for some considerable time. Despite Kizito's continued insistence, Xavier refused to shoot her.

During the genocide, the nuns made little or no effort to conceal their involvement with the militia, as Augustin noted:

> I'm absolutely certain that Kizito never for a minute thought the RPF would defeat the regime. I think that explains her self-assurance and the reason that she advertised her close ties with the militia in such a public manner.

1994 was not the first time that Sr. Kizito had enjoyed close relations with militiamen. She displayed her prejudices and her links to men bent on violence in early 1991 while living in the Benedictine house in Kigufi, Gisenyi. As Gisenyi was Habyarimana's native region, and that of many leading members of the government, tension was exceptionally high in Gisenyi following the RPF invasion in October 1990. It was the Tutsis living in Gisenyi and Ruhengeri who were the first to be killed and threatened as "accomplices" of the RPF. Former employees of the Benedictines living in Kigufi at the time, Hutu as well as Tutsi, found it difficult to comprehend Kizito's behaviour. Théodore Ngororabanga said he tried to talk sense to Kizito, but in vain.

> All the nuns were together—Paula, Agnès, Annonciata and Kizito. When the militia reached the gate, the nuns were shaking in fear and fled to their rooms. But, strangely, Sr. Kizito went to join the militia at the gate. I went to warn her about the risk she was running, but she wouldn't listen to me. Instead,

---

[33] The génocidaires did not, in general, hesitate to kill mentally disturbed Tutsis, as the massacre on 18 April 1994 at the principal psychiatric hospital, Caraes in Ndera, shows.

she just laughed and made fun of me, making me realise how little she was worried about what might happen. I must admit that she was letting the militia in on some secrets. Ignoring what I had told her, Kizito went and talked to the militia for a good twenty minutes. It was quite obvious that she felt at home in their company. After chatting to her, they gave her a *massue*, and left. I don't know what they talked about. When she came, she was carrying the *massue*. I was outside the door of the convent. I could see the militia heading for the health centre where the medical assistant, Bénôit, was a Tutsi. I recognised some of the militiamen, namely Surwumwe's son, Burasanzwe, who is now in prison in Gisenyi; and Ntembako's son, Sikubwabo.

When Kizito arrived carrying her *massue*, she found us near the kitchen. I was with some other employees, namely, Jonas Hitiyaremye, Théoneste Munyakayanza, etc. Our Tutsi friends, including Jean-Marie-Vianney Munyagisenyi, and the other nuns, had gone into hiding.

Kizito was bashing the concrete door beside us and saying: "Today we're going to wipe them out! No-one will ever hear of them again! Where are those *Inyenzi* hiding? They should come out of hiding and show themselves in public as Tutsis! We'll see where they'll run to then". She made these remarks and others in my presence. She was very sure of herself, full of courage and energy when she talked like that, hitting the concrete floor with the *massue*. She acted with the strength of a man.

Meanwhile, her fellow-Sisters were afraid to be seen. She was walking around by herself and confiding in us. When she saw that there was no response from any of us, she went quiet. It was only later that the Tutsi nuns—Annonciata, Vérédiane, and Thérèse—and the Tutsi employees—Jean-Marie-Vianney Munyagisenyi and Jonas Gasigwa—came out of hiding. Annonciata asked Agnès, a westerner, to call the gendarmerie to come and protect them. Some Tutsi women and children had tried to enter the convent, as the situation outside was so dangerous. They included Augustin Ngirinshuti's wife, Marcelline, among others. Sr. Kizito told them to go back home. They did go home, because Kizito was brandishing her *massue* and they were afraid she would hit them with it.

When I asked Kizito why the militia had come here. She replied: "Who else do you think they were looking for except those *Inyenzi*? They should get out. Why are they hiding when it's all over for them?" She added that even she had become an interahamwe. That was a very serious thing to say, when you consider the situation that we were involved in. And then she had a *massue* just like the militia men. How could one think that she meant no harm? Besides, Kizito was always going out to chat to the militia men. She used to buy them *musululu* (sorghum) at Sebisusa's.[34]

Jean Marie-Vianney Munyagisenyi, was one of the employees who went into hiding.

From where I was in the laundry building, I could hear Sr. Kizito making rude remarks about us. She was calling us *Inyenzi*. She told us not to hide, but to come out and take on the militia since we thought we were so strong. She was sure they would wipe us out. She said: *"akabo kashobotse*, meaning "their problem has been settled."

Yet some of her Tutsi fellow-nuns were facing the same danger as us. It was hard to understand how a nun could say such things at such a stressful time for us. I only came out from there later, once the gendarmes were there to reassure us.[35]

Thomas Nyandwi was a regular visitor to the Benedictine house and was there the day the militiamen gave a *massue* to Sr. Kizito.

I found that the nuns were in hiding while Kizito was chatting with the militiamen at the gate. I didn't understand what was going on. I asked Théodore, their worker, what was happening and he told me that he himself didn't understand anything. When I was in the bar in the evening, I heard that the militiamen had given a *massue* to Sr. Kizito that she was using to intimidate her Tutsi fellow-nuns who were in hiding, as well the Tutsi workers such as Jean Marie-Vianney and Jonas. That didn't surprise me because only a few days before that, Kizito had told me that whoever didn't follow the recommendations of MRND was going to have problems and would only have himself to blame.[36]

---

[34] Interviewed in Kigufi, 28 July 1999.
[35] Interviewed in Kigufi, 29 July 1999.
[36] Interviewed in Kigufi, 28 July 1999.

So many people observed the good relations between the two nuns and the militia, that it is impossible to see how Sr. Gertrude would support the claim she has made on Belgium television that "the militia completely despised us and crushed us. We felt completely helpless; We were outcasts."[37] Moreover, the leader of the militia Emmanuel Rekeraho accuses the nuns of playing a vital role in the genocide in Sovu. His evidence is damning. He confirms that they both supported the efforts of the militia wholeheartedly and were under no pressure from the killers. According to Rekeraho, it was only during the genocide that he became close to Sr. Gertrude and Sr. Kizito and that their alliance was founded not on friendship, but on a mutual ambition to eliminate the Tutsi population of Sovu.

> Although they did not use weapons to kill people, Sr. Gertrude and Sr. Kizito got the Tutsis out of their hiding places and handed them over to us. Those two nuns collaborated with us in everything we did. They shared our hatred for the Tutsis. I did not do anything without first discussing it with Kizito and Gertrude. They handed over innocent people, without being threatened in any way, and without us having to use force. They will never be able to prove that they handed people over because they feared for their lives. In our culture, when a hunted animal seeks refuge in the village, it can no longer be killed. But the nuns handed over innocent people who had sought refuge with them. Every time that I went to ask Gertrude and Kizito to give me Tutsis to deliver to the militia, they did it without hesitating for a single second. And yet they were not under threat. They handed over most of the Tutsi workers of the monastery themselves. There are many rooms in the monastery; there is the enclosure and there are the bushes. Why didn't these two nuns hide anyone?
>
> I have heard that the nuns are denying responsibility. I'm ashamed for them. If God let me meet them face to face, I'd see whether they could deny what happened at Sovu.[38]

Charles Butera's wife and children were among the victims on 6 May. Charles, who works in a bank in Kigali, was in Burundi during the genocide. Unable to comprehend her behaviour, he sent a fax to Sr. Gertrude in Belgium.

> It is with great consternation and extreme desolation that I learnt you played an active role in the genocide which ravaged Rwanda.
>
> How could you think of leaving, at the mercy of criminals, a crowd of innocent people who thought of looking to you for refuge and protection?
>
> How did you dare to hand over to the executioners my little Crispin (18 months) who smiled at you innocently and who held out his arms to you, crying "Aunt" and "Jesus" while kissing your cross. You remember that the only four words which until then came out of his mouth were papa, mama, aunt and Jesus. And his mother, Chantal, my very beloved wife, for whom Sovu had become her second family? Did they die from machetes, bullets or clubs? You, and your accomplice, Jonathan Ruremesha, must one day give me explanations.
>
> At the moment, all the survivors spend their days burying the remains of their people. Me, I have criss-crossed the whole country and I have not yet been able to find the remains of my family, so well-prepared was your macabre plan.
>
> My anguish is so immense I cannot find the words to express it. In short, I hold a grudge against you. I dare to hope that we will meet one day, on earth or beneath it, in heaven or in hell. We will have things to explain to each other.

---

[37] Sr. Gertrude made this claim in 1995 during an interview with the Belgian television station, RBTF; see below for details.

[38] Interviewed in Kigali 24 May and 7 July 1999.

Faith in Falsehoods
Help from the Catholic Church in Belgium

"The religious authorities in Belgium did not even take the trouble to establish the truth about what happened in Sovu."

On 1 July, fighting between government soldiers and the RPF reached the outskirts of Butare town, not far from the Benedictine monastery. It was decided that the nuns of Sovu and other members of the clergy should be evacuated to the former Zaire. Mgr. Jean-Baptiste Gahamanyi, then Bishop of the Diocese of Butare, invited them to stay at the bishopric, from where they would begin their journey. The fact that Rekeraho led the convoy of cars taking the nuns to the bishopric, speaks volumes about the strength of the Mother Superior's relationship with the militiaman. Annonciata Mukagasana described their journey.

> Rekeraho himself came to collect us that evening. We could already hear gunfire and assumed it was the RPF. Rekeraho had the ambulance; Sr. Gertrude was driving a Mazda and Sr. Stéphanie was driving a Volkswagen. Rekeraho headed the convoy. We were not harassed at the roadblocks; Rekeraho had probably given them advance warning.

Because they were a large group, some of the clergy were housed at the bishopric and others went to the African Catechist Institute. Arrangements had been made for French soldiers—who had arrived in Rwanda to establish Zone Turquoise—to escort them as far as Gikongoro. The two groups were to meet up at the bishopric on 3 July and to leave together from there. But the nuns and priests who were at the bishopric left early. They were following a truck of French soldiers, but on the way they must have lost sight of them. They were ambushed by militiamen and killed at Ndago, commune Mubuga in Gikongoro. The victims included nine nuns from Sovu and several priests.

The remaining nuns went on to Gikongoro as planned. Then after four days, French soldiers took them to Zaire. They spent a month at the convent of the Trappistine Sisters in Muresha, before moving to Goma and then on to Bangui in the Central African Republic. In Bangui, the nuns had their first opportunity to talk to outsiders about their experiences in Rwanda. But Sr. Gertrude made every effort to cut them off from the outside world, as Annonciata recalled.

> We met some Tutsi families in Bangui, working for UNDP. They were Sebera, Marthe and others. They wanted to get together with us to raise our morale and to find out what really happened in Rwanda. But Gertrude categorically refused to let us talk to them. I remember Marthe asking us why we were going to France when we ought to be going home to Rwanda. We didn't know what to say.

However, as Marie-Bernard pointed out, Sr. Gertrude publicised her own version of what took place at the monastery from April-July 1994 in the French newspaper, *La Croix.*

> When we were in Bangui, Sr. Gertrude gave false information to the newspaper, *La Croix,* which appalled us more than ever. She boasted of a bravery she had never shown. It was in August 1994 that her article appeared in *La Croix.* It made us really angry. She said we were all united and had all asked forgiveness of each other.

After a short time in Bangui, the nuns went to France and then to Belgium, arriving in Maredret on 16 August. The principal Benedictine abbey in Belgium is in Maredret, in the region of Namur, Flanders, described by one observer as the "stronghold of Flemish Catholicism." [39] The Benedictine nuns from Kigufi in Gisenyi were also evacuated to Belgium.

---

[39] "Blood Sisters", Philip Jacobson, *Sunday Times Magazine,* 28 January 1996.

In Belgium, Sr. Gertrude's position as the Mother Superior gave her considerable influence over the fate of her community. She used this influence to restrict the movements of the other nuns and to prevent them from speaking to outsiders. She even sought to stop the Sovu nuns from communicating with each other. In the words of one nun, "in Maredret, we were always locked up in the convent." Annonciata expressed similar frustrations.

> When we arrived in Belgium, Gertrude not only forbade us to talk to anyone outside, but she even stopped us—the Tutsi sisters—from communicating amongst ourselves. I recall Kizito coming and eavesdropping while I was answering a phone call from Bangui. Gertrude even ridiculed Sr. Scholastique in our presence, asking her what she had to talk about all the time with the Tutsi novices.

The impact on their lives was considerable, as Marie-Bernard testified.

> To prevent us from denouncing her, once we arrived in Maredret, Gertrude tried to stop us from speaking either to each other or to anyone else. Since we didn't even have our passports, we couldn't move from the abbey in Maredret and were virtually prisoners there.

Because of the circumstances in which they had left Rwanda and arrived in Belgium, the nuns and novices did not have their own passports, except Sr. Béata who had obtained a passport in preparation for studying abroad. This gave Gertrude the power to limit their mobility and to curb their independence. Mélanie, cited above, was a novice at Maredret.

> In Maredret we were really blocked, cut off from any outside communication. Gertrude succeeded in cutting us off because, apart from her, none of the other nuns amongst us had a passport. She had her passport and a piece of paper on which all our names were written by hand. We were like sheep driven out to pasture.
>   The fact that we didn't have passports really limited us. We couldn't leave Maredret without being in Gertrude's company to justify the reasons for our stay in Belgium by presenting her passport. Even to get medical treatment, it was necessary for Gertrude to be there to accompany us.

An acquaintance, who had known the nuns in Rwanda, described the difficult situation in which they found themselves.

> Sr. Gertrude was the only one who came forward to talk. It was impossible to speak to the other nuns. They only turned up to say two words to us: "Hello and goodbye." One could say, without exaggeration, that all the other Benedictine nuns from Sovu and Kigufi had been taken hostage by Gertrude. She didn't want the nuns to leave Maredret for fear that they would talk about their experiences during the genocide. These nuns didn't have any administrative papers to justify their status in Belgium. To see how her colleagues could obtain their passports was the least of Gertrude's concerns. When she sought to have their stay extended, she obliged the rest of the community to follow her to the administrative authorities. That was very awkward because none of them could speak with the Belgian administrative authorities to explain their problem. The attitude of Gertrude ended up by creating a general feeling of unhappiness amongst the other nuns.

After some weeks in Maredret, some of the nuns were transferred to Benedictine houses in Namur, Liège and Rixensart. The nuns who were considered the most critical of Sr. Gertrude were all transferred out of Maredret. Many of the nuns interviewed for this report believe that Sr. Gertrude decided to separate them when she realised that limiting the nuns' access to the outside world would not be sufficient to ensure their silence. Marie-Bernard commented:

> When she realised that things were not going in her favour, Gertrude took steps on 2 September to separate us so that we could not communicate with each other or share our ideas about returning to Rwanda. She sent us off to different Benedictine monasteries, without consulting us.

But whatever Sr. Gertrude's motives for moving the nuns to different convents, her action had consequences she could not have intended, as Mélanie explained.

> For us, there was also a positive aspect to being scattered around; it gave us an opportunity to explain our wish to return to Rwanda to some of our superiors.

The Official Response

The nuns' sense of isolation was reinforced by the treatment they received from the authorities in the Benedictine order and other branches of the Catholic Church. They were never left in any doubt that the Church would support Sr. Gertrude and Sr. Kizito.[40] Even before they reached Belgium, the nuns discovered where the sympathies of their superiors lay. Marie-Bernard said:

> Throughout our long journey, not a single White Father or White Sister had said as much as "I'm sorry" for what had happened to us. On the contrary, they all said to Gertrude: "Poor Gertrude has sweated blood for her community." You could see they all felt sorry for her.

Mélanie described the approach taken by the Benedictine order and certain other clergy to the problem.

> The religious authorities in Belgium did not even take the trouble to establish the truth about what happened in Sovu. They simply wanted to cover up for the Church and protected the individual without knowing her.

She described the tensions at Maredret when they lived there.

> The atmosphere was bad since some of the Sisters in our community didn't want to live with Sr. Gertrude unless she was accused, and if possible, asked forgiveness for all the bad things she did during the genocide. We really wanted to denounce her bad behaviour. But no-one was interested in asking us about it. On the contrary, we saw that the religious authorities were supporting Sr. Gertrude, to such an extent that they told her that they could even set up our community in another African country instead of letting us return to Rwanda.

It soon became clear that Sr. Gertrude had managed to convince the Benedictine hierarchy not only that the allegations of involvement in the genocide were unfounded, but that she had in fact been responsible for saving lives. She had told them her version of events and been believed. There was no attempt on the part of the Church leaders to hear the views of the other nuns.

Keeping the Nuns in Belgium

Shortly after their arrival in Belgium, Sr. Marie-Bernard and Sr. Scholastique expressed their wish to return to Rwanda. But Sr. Gertrude and the Benedictine hierarchy wanted all the nuns to remain in Belgium. They wanted, at all costs, to avoid a situation in which only Sr. Gertrude and Sr. Kizito were left in Belgium, which would inevitably raise questions about their role in the genocide. They argued that Rwanda was unsafe, unstable and that the Hutu nuns were liable to be arrested simply because they were Hutu. The pressure was intense, according to Mélanie.

> They looked for the slightest reason to show that Rwanda was not stable. There were rumours in Belgium according to which Hutus who went back were poisoned. Everyone felt fearful. Even I was

---

[40] In Belgium, the public debate about the Sovu nuns has focused on Sr. Gertrude because of her position as the Mother Superior, because of her willingness to participate in television interviews and because Sr. Kizito does not speak French.

afraid. At the same time, I knew, when I thought about what had happened in Sovu, that I couldn't keep quiet.

The first meeting of the Rwandese nuns and novices in Maredret, on 11 November, was presided over by Abbot Celestine Cullen, the president of the Benedictine Congregation of our Lady, based in Limerick, Ireland. Marie-Bernard recalled his response when she and Scholastique told him that they wanted to leave for Rwanda.

Abbot Cullen was initially in favour of our idea. Later, he changed his mind. He spoke individually with every nun from the community of Sovu and then laid down four conditions for our return to Rwanda:

- Somebody must be willing to take us in Rwanda;
- Somebody must promise to guarantee our safety;
- Somebody must take responsibility for our sustenance such as food, etc;
- We must have permission from our Mother Superior, that is, Gertrude Mukangango.

Marie-Bernard immediately wrote to the Bishop Gahamanyi, asking him for assistance with regard to the first three conditions. He replied positively. The fourth condition was, in the words of Marie-Bernard, "a trap."

What we did not have was Gertrude's permission. That was to be expected since she didn't want to go back to Rwanda. I gave the Bishop of Butare's response to Abbot Cullen; we waited in vain for him to respond.

After the meeting of 11 November, Scholastique and Marie-Bernard contacted both Abbot Cullen and Sr. Gertrude. In a letter dated 28 November, they informed them of their plans to leave for Rwanda. Saying that they had already sent a note to Sr. Gertrude on 19 November, they wrote:

... We are the only community which has not shown a sign of going to our country while all the congregations have sent members to [begin] reconstruction of the Church. Even the Carmelite Sisters who are the most cloistered, like us, are in Kigali. Mgr. Jean-Baptiste Gahamanyi is willing to take responsibility for us... With regard to the conditions discussed during the meeting of 12 November 1994 with the Abbot in Maredret, the only outstanding decision is that of the community. We are very sorry that we cannot wait for it because it is very urgent. We prefer to go there and to keep you informed for the time being. Consequently we are leaving like "the two doves of Noah's Ark", not as the crow. May your blessing accompany us and draw God's blessing towards us.

Marie-Bernard did not allow her exile to Rixensart, or Abbot Cullen's failure to respond, dampen her determination to go back to her homeland. She managed to contact Scholastique by telephone to plan their journey home.

We reiterated our request to Abbot Cullen. But he told us to see Sr. Gertrude, who said she could not see anyone before Christmas 1994. Scholastique and I wrote to Fr. Cullen to tell him we were going back to Rwanda before December. He threatened not to give us the tickets we needed to return. He asked us where we thought we would otherwise get tickets. He thought we didn't know anyone else who could help us.

The two nuns found Belgian friends willing to pay for their journey to Rwanda. With their tickets in their hands, they made their arrangements in secret. Their contacts also helped them to obtain the necessary passports from the Rwandese embassy in Belgium. On 30 November, they arrived at Brussels airport; an hour before the plane was due to leave, they telephoned Maredret and Rixensart to inform their colleagues of their decision. Marie-Bernard recalled the last-minute attempt by the Church authorities to prevent their departure to Rwanda.

The White Fathers and Benedictine Sisters of Maredret did everything they could to get the police to stop us from going back. But it was too late. When the police arrived, we were already on the aeroplane.

Sr. Scholastique and Sr. Marie-Bernard arrived at the bishopric of Butare on 4 December 1994. It was a complicated homecoming—relief and joy mingled with grief, sadness and fear of what the future held.

The departure of Scholastique and Marie-Bernard was a severe setback for Sr. Gertrude, as Annonciata Mukagasana discovered.

Their decision threw Gertrude into panic. She had been busy encouraging us to remain in Belgium. Gertrude said that she would ask for Belgian citizenship. I myself felt that I couldn't stay in Europe for very long. Gertrude encouraged me to become a novice in Belgium, but I didn't feel strong enough to begin life as a nun under those circumstances. I asked to return to Rwanda. She begged me to stay in Europe, but I refused. I didn't know whether my family was still alive. A week before I left, someone phoned me and told me that my family was living in Kigali.

Control and Containment

The sudden departure of Sr. Marie-Bernard and Sr. Scholastique forced the Benedictine community in Belgium to confront the ongoing conflicts within the Sovu community. Worried that others may follow their example, the Mother Superior of Maredret recalled the other Rwandese nuns to Maredret, except Sr. Cécile and Sr. Solange who were studying in Namur. Long before Scholastique and Marie-Bernard left for Rwanda, the Benedictine authorities in Belgium knew that nuns from Sovu had accused Sr. Gertrude and Sr. Kizito of collusion in the genocide. But although the accusations came from within their own order, the Benedictines dismissed them. However, after the two nuns returned to Rwanda, it became impossible to keep the lid on the allegations. In the course of 1995, survivors came forward to accuse Sr. Gertrude and Sr. Kizito of supporting the genocide in Sovu, and it became apparent that they were wanted for questioning by the authorities in Rwanda. The Belgian press reported the story, sending shockwaves through the Benedictine order.

Despite the strength of the charges against the Sisters, the order offered them wholehearted and unwavering support. In an interview with a Belgian journalist on 13 February 1995, Sr. Marie-Jeanne, aged 82 at the time, summed up their position. Sr. Marie-Jeanne had once been head of the Benedictine order in Rwanda, but she was evacuated from Sovu on 18 April, and so was absent during the killings.

Saying that Gertrude was "exhausted" and "terribly shaken by all the events since the month of April", Sr. Marie-Jeanne said that Gertrude had left for "a week of complete rest." She said that Gertrude was "managing to overcome it, little by little" but that her recovery "isn't easy."

She [Gertrude] did everything she could to defend the others at our [convent] in Sovu. She even paid them to spare the Sisters' families. But they took the money and killed them anyway.

The journalist asked her to explain the reasons for the "tension" between the Rwandese nuns to which Sr. Marie-Jeanne had alluded.

Because family members were killed. And the Sisters thought that the Superior could have done more to save them. But that is wrong. She really did everything she could. But at a certain time, the interahamwe arrived, saying that as they were sheltering Tutsis, they were going to kill everybody, including the Sisters. And so it was the bourgmestre, I think, and yet another important person who said: Sister Gertrude, it will serve no purpose to keep the guests. They have to leave or else they will certainly kill you all. She felt responsible for the community [of Sisters] above all else, for the 35 Sisters who were there. And so she asked the guests to leave. We had about 60 guests and amongst them were family members who had come for refuge. So she asked everyone to leave. She really did it to save the Sisters' lives...[O]n the question of Gertrude, I would personally prefer that there was no publicity. I hope things will settle down.

With Gertrude, these are complaints from people who believed that their family could have been saved and it is being repeated. You know how Rwanda is and especially now... It seems that denunciations are made to settle scores. And then you are put in prison where you stay and there is no justice.

Sr. Marie-Jeanne's interview demonstrates blind faith in the nuns; the limits of her own perceptions of the situation in Rwanda; and concern about the repercussions the affair could have upon the order's image. It soon became evident that the rest of the Benedictines would take a similar approach.

Undue Pressure

Without any independent knowledge of what had occurred in Sovu during the genocide, the Benedictines saw fit to act as judge and jury and to declare the innocence of Sr. Gertrude and Sr. Kizito. They began to prepare a defence on behalf of Sr. Gertrude. But the fact that many of the other Sovu nuns were aware of what had happened at the monastery during the genocide presented a problem. Fr. André Comblin, a White Father who had lived in Rwanda, was asked to organise a seminar for the nuns in Ermeton, in the Liège region. Although he is not a Benedictine, it was thought that his knowledge of Rwanda would be an asset in defusing the situation. For the first time, the nuns were given an opportunity to voice their concerns. Each Sister was asked to speak freely and to say what she thought about the rumours that their order was divided. Yvonne[41], one of the nuns who took part in the meeting, described the exchange.

We noted that there was no division in the community, [but] rather that the problem lay in the refusal of certain Sisters, who had conducted themselves badly in the genocide, to return to Rwanda. Sr. Libérata Nirere accused Gertrude of behaving badly during the genocide. She said that Gertrude had handed over a young boy that she, Libérata, had hidden in the ceiling. Libérata had been giving him food and drink. She had given him instructions so that he would know it was her. She would come below the place where the boy was hiding and, on hearing her noise, the boy would appear. One unfortunate day, Gertrude passed below [his place of hiding] and the boy made a mistake, thinking it was Libérata who was bringing something for him. He appeared and Gertrude made him come down and chased him out of the monastery. That boy was killed. Libérata added that this boy's presence wasn't bothering anyone, especially since it was a time when almost all the Tutsis of Sovu had already been massacred.

Gertrude also faced other accusations.

Gertrude had also refused to welcome the relatives of our nuns.

Sr. Gertrude did not offer any remorse or explanation.

Gertrude lowered her head during this meeting and said that [these accusations] were not true.

It was clear from this meeting that several of the Sovu nuns were not prepared to support their Mother Superior and that more would have to be done to convince them to do so.

---

[41] This is a pseudonym.

Eliciting False Statements

The Benedictines took advantage of the confusion and insecurity felt by the nuns. The threat of expulsion hung over Sr. Scholastique and Sr. Marie Bernard because it was thought that they had spoken out against the Mother Superior, and the rest of the nuns were made to feel it was their duty to support her. Pressurising the nuns in this manner was more than just meddling on the part of the Church, given the serious nature of the charges; it amounts to obstruction of justice. Mélanie took part in a second retreat organised by Fr. Comblin in Ermeton; this time, he invited Fr. Nicolas Dayez, a Benedictine priest at Maredsous. He was an assistant to Abbot Cullen and often acted as his representative in what came to be known as "the Sovu affair."

> After Scholastique and Marie Bernard went back to Rwanda, the situation became almost disastrous. The religious authorities gathered us together to decide to expel Sister Scholastique and Marie-Bernard from the community. That was their wish. At the head of these religious authorities were Abbot Celestine, Fr. Nicolas Dayez, a Benedictine priest from the community in Maredsous and Fr. André Comblin, who was supposed to know more about the problems in Rwanda than the other White Fathers as he had lived there a long time.
>
> Fr. Comblin seemed to say that the problems of our community were political problems of an ethnic nature. He didn't want to go into the heart of the problem; he went all around the issue. The next day, he began the retreat by telling us that the two disobedient Sisters, Marie-Bernard and Scholastique, had, before they left, accused their colleague, Sister Gertrude, of participating in the genocide. Fr. Comblin said that it was necessary to neutralise these false accusations by giving positive testimonies absolving Sister Gertrude.
>
> After he had said this, nearly all the Sisters were shocked because not one of us knew anything about it. He went on to regroup the Sisters in small numbers, to control them better, I think, and to force them to give the testimonies he mentioned. He did this step by step. Sr. Libérata Nirere refused to comply. Libérata said that it was Sr. Gertrude who, instead, should ask for pardon for her bad behaviour during the genocide. Sr. Libérata said: "Not only have you hurt the refugees. But you have also hurt your fellow Sisters whose relatives had taken refuge in our monastery." Comblin didn't want Sr. Libérata to continue describing what Gertrude had done during the genocide. He simply cut her off from speaking. Solange also refused to testify on behalf of Gertrude. She said that it wouldn't be of any use to say good things about Sr. Gertrude, without also talking about her inhumane behaviour. She added that she hadn't seen her good side. Comblin handed out pieces of paper so that the Sisters could write their testimonies on behalf of Sr. Gertrude. We didn't know what the others wrote since it was secret.

Yvonne, one of the nuns pressured into writing a false testimony, recalled the orders they were given.

> One day all the nuns and novices of Sovu were obliged to give written testimonies saying that Sr. Gertrude had behaved well during the genocide. We were asked to say all the good acts of Gertrude during the genocide.
>
> This obligation came from a nun, Löise, originally Swiss, and mother superior of the Benedictine Sisters of Ermeton. All the Sisters and novices wrote about the good acts of Gertrude, except Libérata and Solange who refused.

Yvonne highlighted the considerable influence which the Benedictines were able to exploit in favour of Sr. Gertrude and Sr. Kizito.

> Some Sisters like Löise have acquaintances everywhere. Löise knows a woman who works in the judicial system in Belgium. It is this woman who helps her in camouflaging the nasty role of Kizito and Gertrude. This woman works in Brussels. Löise also gave her all the false texts in order to support Gertrude.
>
> There is a letter that Fr. Nicolas demanded that Gertrude write to the secretary of the King of Belgium.

The two nuns who had refused to write false testimonies, Sr. Libérata Nirere and Sr. Solange Uwanyirigira, were summoned to Brussels by officials in the judiciary. Despite the pressure, they refused to deny what had happened at Sovu.

Although some nuns were persuaded to testify on behalf of Sr. Gertrude, they would not agree to the expulsion of Sr. Scholastique and Sr. Marie Bernard. A meeting was organised in Maredret, together with the Benedictine nuns from Kigufi, to encourage the nuns to agree to the expulsion. Mélanie explained that Sr. Gertrude gave the nuns a choice:

> On this occasion we had to vote for the expulsion of Scholastique and Marie Bernard from our community since they had left without permission. Gertrude spoke. She said that Scholastique had always been jealous of her, that what she wanted was to replace her since, even in Rwanda, she had been trying to be very nice to the novices. We wondered if being nice was a shortcoming. In any case, novices did not vote for the Mother Superior.
>
> Gertrude concluded by saying that she was going to resign if her fellow Sisters weren't expelled. It was a way of showing that her threat should not be taken lightly so that the White Fathers, who were present, should find a way to make things turn in Gertrude's favour.

> A secret ballot was organised to determine the vote.

> Unfortunately for Sr. Gertrude, all the Sisters understood why Scholastique and Marie-Bernard left without permission. They hoped that these Sisters would be re-integrated into the community in Belgium and so avoid the brutal decision to dismiss them.

> The outcome left bitter feelings.

> Gertrude could not bear her defeat and she left her position as Mother Superior. The religious authorities were not happy. But they couldn't do otherwise, considering the results of the vote. They had to content themselves with telling us that the community is like a family, that when something isn't going well, it was important to fix it from within, without going outside it. It was a way of telling us that we shouldn't reveal anything to anybody.

Sr. Gertrude spoke to a Belgian television station on the day of her resignation. With the help of two other interviewees, she sought to present her own version of what happened in Sovu during the genocide. It is difficult to relate any aspect of her account to the evidence given by the nuns, militiamen or by the survivors of Sovu. Sr. Gertrude tries to represent herself and the other nuns as among the primary targets of the militiamen and to argue that her own life was constantly under threat during the genocide. She argues that rather than turning refugees away from the monastery, she was hoping they would escape.

Sister Gertrude's Account

On the day she resigned in early 1995, Sr. Gertrude gave a detailed interview to a Belgian television programme entitled "Le Coeur et L'Esprit" where she insists that the nuns were thought of as "RPF accomplices... a target for troublemakers." Contrary to the many testimonies which highlight Sr. Gertrude's refusal to allow Tutsis to enter the monastery, in the interview she claims that she had been "sheltering" the refugees who were massacred on the 22nd. Speaking of her decision to take the nuns to the Parish of Ngoma on 23rd, the day after the massacre at the health centre, she said it was because the "nuns were to have been massacred the day after." Yet, Sr. Gertrude does not explain how she felt able to ask one of the leading organisers of the genocide in Huye commune, the bourgmestre, Jonathan Ruremesha, to accompany them to the parish.

Sr. Gertrude then claims that she took the nuns back to Sovu because they "preferred to die in our own church." And she gives the following account of the treatment they received from Rekeraho, the leader of the militia, when they arrived.

Father André Comblin

Sister Gertrude: When we got there, the militia leader decided that the execution would take place the next day, and gave us one night to prepare for death.

The Presenter: Were you the only one who knew that, or did all the nuns know?

Sister Gertrude: When we arrived, the militiaman took me aside, and told me he was going to execute us the next day. I didn't tell the other nuns about it immediately but waited until midnight and we prayed. It was a terrible ordeal. We asked for forgiveness for ourselves and for them. We prayed for our executioners, and we were ready to meet our God.

The Presenter: That must indeed have been a time of great, even intense suffering?

Sister Gertrude: It was a strange time; acceptance of an unjust death and also the joy of going to join our Creator. We were radiant and ready to die. We had closed the chapter of our previous lives.

The Presenter: And the next morning?

Sister Gertrude: Next morning, we went down to our church, which we had left after the attacks, to die there. When the militia arrived, we went. I went and opened the door myself, together with another Sister. Then they asked me to go to the hostelry. They had a list they had drawn up in our absence, and they called people there, and they subjected me to a long interrogation.

Although in fact there was never any attempt on the part of the militia to kill the nuns, the massacre of 25 April led to the death of a number of Tutsis who had managed to hide in the monastery. Sr. Gertrude gave this description of what happened that day and in the weeks that followed.

> I said that I wasn't in contact with the RPF, but he [the militiaman] insisted that I was. He said he'd have me prosecuted, and he made everyone come out, saying he was going to drive them to the commune office. He got everyone out like that and, instead of driving them to the commune office as he'd said, he executed them, and told me we'd be executed that afternoon...
>
> After that, we just waited until the afternoon. He came back and told me it would be tomorrow. We tried to resist them, but not aggressively because they were very strong. We tried to resist gently, which we could do, and we held out until May with all the people they had spared, and no-one came to our aid then. They went on threatening us and finally they put us up against the wall and had decided to execute us. Then, at that very moment, instead of all of us dying together, we tried to get away from there. There are some people who left, and I'm accused of letting them leave whereas I was trying to save their lives.

Sr. Gertrude is accused of having called the militia to kill the nuns' relatives on 6 May. The interviewer asked her if it was true that she had "let these refugees leave," that she was "leading them to certain death." Sr. Gertrude gave the following response.

> I hoped they'd escape being killed if they left, because until then, all the ones I'd sheltered had been killed. Nothing could persuade me that they'd be safe, especially as we were surrounded by the militia who were ready to massacre all of us along with them... When I decided they should leave, I was hoping help might arrive... I intended to save people but, as the country was in a terrible state, no-one wanted other people to survive. Well, some of those people were not protected. I hoped they'd be protected and get some help; that was what I wanted. Deciding they should stay meant deciding they should die. When I decided they should leave, I was hoping help might arrive.[42]

Sr. Gertrude claims to have forgiven her accusers and to understand why they spoke out against her:

---

[42] "Le Coeur et L'Esprit", shown on RTBF in 1995.

Father Martin Neyt

These charges against me are false because they attribute to me intentions I never had. The militia completely despised us and crushed us. We felt completely helpless; We were outcasts. When I think about these people making the accusations, I remind myself that they've been traumatised. They thought I could do amazing things when it was quite impossible.

Sr. Gertrude's explanations were supported by Fr. Martin Neyt, a representative of the Benedictine Order in Belgium. He said:

I have come here first of all as a brother, a Benedictine brother, coming to support an African sister, but at the same time, our Benedictine order has given me a mandate to make certain facts known. I'd also like to set the record straight regarding the coverage by the press and the mass media... It seems to me there have been a lot of things left out, a lot of simplification and a lot of incorrect elements in recent reports. And it seems to me that one could ask those responsible to check their facts more thoroughly and provide more information, instead of competing for the best scandal...

Fr. Neyt then spoke about the statements the nuns had been asked to write in favour of Sr. Gertrude.

Because the facts are very important. Lives are at stake. So what I'd like to say is that the head of our Order has questioned all the Sisters in that community, and we have seven written statements, including one from a Tutsi, a community elder. All the younger ones have testified that not only has Sr. Gertrude done nothing to merit any of the criticism made against her, but on the contrary, she gave people food and helped them. She even helped some people escape. She did everything to help both her community and the refugees, and I think she found herself faced with a dilemma...

The dead have an important place in these communities, and so one can understand how some Sisters were traumatised by the deaths of their loved ones and over-reacted a bit. But our Order is paying no attention to these reactions, whereas the written and signed statements by the Sisters are being taken seriously, and can be brought in to confirm the truth of the Sister's own statement.

Speaking of her decision to resign, Sr. Gertrude said:

I resigned today to allow my Sisters to go home to Rwanda with a different Mother Superior. Because now I've been accused, I'm afraid to go back to my country, my life is in danger.

Sr. Gertrude's resignation was interpreted as a further instance of her "suffering." Abbot Cullen wrote to Bishop Gahamanyi on 6 April 1995. He explained why he had felt "great sadness" in accepting the resignation of Sr. Gertrude as Mother Superior.

Mother Gertrude deserves everyone's admiration on account of the courage that she showed in confronting the terrible events and which enabled her to save the life of her community, in every sense of the word. It is clear that my acceptance of this resignation does not in any way mean that I approve of the attitude of Sisters Scholastique and Marie-Bernard, who have committed serious errors in the manner of their behaviour. My acceptance is even less a sign that I attach any substance to the accusations against Mother Gertrude according to which she participated in the genocide.

Sr. Anastasie Mukamusoni was chosen to replace Sr. Gertrude as the new Mother Superior.
At the end of August 1995, there was extensive publicity in Belgium about the alleged role of Sr. Gertrude and Sr. Kizito in the genocide, following a documentary by BBC Television and the publication of a report by African Rights, *Rwanda: Not So Innocent, When Women Become Killers.* On 31 August, Sr. Gertrude spoke with a journalist from RTBF television. Asked to explain why she was being accused of supporting the genocide in Sovu, she gave this response.

It's surprising that people can actually say it. But, I think [it comes from] some people who have been hurt, or else who find themselves in a situation that I don't know about. I am in Europe, I don't know in what context that is happening, why they are doing it and what they want. I cannot therefore explain why [there is] this campaign against me when I really tried to protect the people with all the means at my disposal. [I was] a poor woman who had no means of resisting, faced with an evil force which was stronger than me.

With regard to the accusations, I haven't seen one testimony which agrees with the other. Each time it's something different. The first time it was the families of the nuns. The second time, there was an article saying that when the refugees came, I treated them in a scornful manner... It's all a complete fabrication.

Sr. Gertrude laid the blame on Sr. Scholastique and Marie-Bernard.

When the first two nuns returned to Rwanda, well, they began to spread the rumour that I am responsible for the death of their brothers... Fr. Nicolas went to meet them. I was ready to go to meet them [and] to ask them: But how is that possible? We made the journey together, we lived here as a united group, how has it happened that you have suddenly come out with that? We could have seen him together..., but as they had repeated [the story] in Rwanda, I was told: "No, if you come to Rwanda, you will be imprisoned."

As an alternative to Rwanda, some of the senior Belgian nuns proposed establishing a house in Belgium for the Rwandese nuns. But the new Rwandese Mother Superior, Sr. Anastasie Mukamusoni, convinced that their future lay in Rwanda, set out to organise their return in a discreet manner. In addition to mobilising the other nuns, she made arrangements to obtain their passports through the Rwandese embassy in Brussels, without the knowledge of their order in Belgium. Alarmed, the Benedictine order tried to discourage the nuns, saying that their security in Rwanda could not be guaranteed. In another effort to prolong their stay in Belgium, they argued that Rwanda had become an "Anglophone country" and offered the nuns courses in English. It was eventually agreed that the new Mother Superior would visit Rwanda to judge the situation for herself. She left together with some of the elderly nuns who had made up their minds to leave for Rwanda. On her return, she reported that the situation was calm. She also made it clear that she planned to transfer the community back to Rwanda. All the nuns agreed to settle in Rwanda, except Sr. Gertrude and Sr. Kizito.

In Pursuit of Lies

"The truth is that Sr. Gertrude personally opened the monastery to welcome the refugees. With other Sisters, she took care to ensure that they were given food and treatment. She even helped some of them to escape."

The Benedictines continued their efforts to suppress the truth about the genocide in Sovu by pursuing Sr. Scholastique and Sr. Marie Bernard to Rwanda. They blamed the two nuns for informing the media in Belgium, and the government in Rwanda, about the role of Sr. Gertrude and Sr. Kizito in the genocide. The Church put intense pressure upon them to deny their stories and, when this failed, it treated them as outcasts. The suffering Sr. Scholastique and Sr. Marie-Bernard experienced as a result of the genocide, has been deepened by the treatment they received from the Church.

After Marie-Bernard and Scholastique arrived in Rwanda, they were obliged to settle at the bishopric in Butare because of an order from Maredret that banned them from entering the monastery in Sovu. At the time, the monastery was occupied by a non-governmental organisation, Terre des hommes, which was looking after unaccompanied children there. Marie-Bernard and Scholastique expressed the wish to live in the monastery and to take up the activity of making communion wafers. They visited the monastery on 12 December 1994, a week after their return to Rwanda, saying that they had come at the request of Bishop Gahamanyi. But Terre des hommes refused to allow them back into the monastery, arguing that the premises had been lent to them by Sr. Gertrude in a letter sent from Belgium on 23 October. Watchmen were placed at the entrance to prevent them from entering the premises. Terre des hommes sent a fax to Sr. Gertrude on the day of their visit, asking for guidance. Sr. Gertrude responded the same day, saying that "having detached themselves from the community, Sisters Scholastique and Marie-Bernard know that the monastery doesn't belong to them anymore." Emphasising the "blatant disobedience" of Scholastique and Marie-Bernard in coming back to Rwanda without official permission, other members of the Benedictine order, including Abbot Celestine Cullen and Fr. Nicolas Dayez, wrote in support of the position taken by Sr. Gertrude. They added that she had the right to take the decision on behalf of their community, even though she was in exile.

The bishopric of Butare wanted to recuperate the building, to have the children housed elsewhere and also wanted Scholastique and Marie-Bernard to have access to the monastery. Furthermore, it disputed the right of Sr. Gertrude to decide the fate of the monastery while in exile. In a letter dated 13 December, Bishop Gahamanyi informed Terre des hommes of his plans for the two nuns.

> I would like the two nuns who have come back to the country to have access to the hostelry workshop with its annexes.

Terre des hommes again appealed to Sr. Gertrude in Maredret, sending her a fax there on 18 December. A Belgian nun, Sr. Marie-Jeanne, wrote to Bishop Gahamanyi, saying that Sr. Gertrude agreed with her response.

> I must first of all inform you that the two nuns who are in Butare returned there without the knowledge of their community... It is a case of blatant disobedience which we cannot take lightly and it is the reason why we cannot allow them to settle in Sovu since they cut themselves off from their community.
>
> We understand very well your desire to see that the equipment at the monastery are used, but you will certainly understand that the case is too serious, from the perspective of religious life and its demands, for us to agree to this wish, and thereby justify the conduct of the two Sisters.

Sr. Marie-Jeanne added:

There must be equipment in Kigali and in Remera which is not being used. If you can make it available to them, the Sisters could make a contribution there.

Bishop Gahamanyi wrote a second letter on 24 January 1995, again requesting Terre des hommes to vacate the monastery. A meeting took place on 15 February to resolve the deadlock. Fr. Nicolas Dayez travelled from Belgium to represent the Benedictines; Mgr. Félicien Mubiligi, the vicar-general of the diocese of Butare, represented Bishop Gahamanyi. Other participants included staff from Terre des hommes and the relevant government ministries.

Fr. Dayez: The two Sisters left Belgium without the permission of their superiors. Therefore they don't have the right to be the first to enter [the monastery].

Mgr. Mubiligi: We are all waiting to know the law which prevents them from going to their home.

Straton Nsanzabaganwa, an official of the Ministry of Labour and Social Affairs and the chairman of the meeting, commented:

According to Rwandese custom, a member of a family which has become dispersed can always return to the paternal residence on their own and before the others, without any kind of ban.

But Fr. Dayez was adamant that the two Sisters had forfeited the right to reside in the monastery. The discussion quickly turned to the question of Sr. Gertrude and her refusal to return to Rwanda. Fr. Dayez gave this explanation for her reluctance to leave Belgium for Rwanda.

Sr. Gertrude knows, since a month, that she is accused of having participated in the genocide, of allowing the families of her fellow-nuns to be massacred [but if she had not done this] the entire community would have been killed.

Fr. Dayez also insisted that Sr. Gertrude had the right to take a decision binding on the monastery "for at least a year." Scholastique and Marie-Bernard were also interviewed and their views included in the records of the meeting. They said that according to the rules and constitution of their order, Sr. Gertrude should have consulted them before she loaned the monastery to Terre des hommes. They dismissed the argument of Fr. Dayez that they did not have to be consulted because they had "disobeyed" their order. They pointed out that she had made the decision in October 1994 when they were still living in Belgium under her supervision. They did not, in any case, believe that they had been disobedient. Scholastique said that she had "decided to return to Rwanda to reconstruct the country and the Church. We wanted to work; we were not disobedient." Marie-Bernard expressed a similar opinion.

I wrote a letter to the Mother Superior, Gertrude, to seek her permission to come back to Rwanda, but she did not reply to me... I didn't understand why we were prevented from coming back to our country when several foreign clergymen have returned.[43]

The meeting decided that Marie-Bernard and Scholastique had "the right to go back to their house (the monastery) like all the other recent refugees [who] return to their residence when they come back to the country."[44] But it was not the end of the matter. A few weeks later, the Vatican intervened. In a letter written on 8 March to Bishop Gahamanyi, Secretary Francisco Javier Errazuriz Ossa asked the bishop to allow Terre des hommes to remain at the monastery until October. He also referred to the wider problems.

---

[43] Cited in the minutes of the meeting, dated 17 February 1995.
[44] *Ibid.*

Fr. Dayez tells us that after his visit, the Mother Superior, Sr. Gertrude—in a sorry state physically and psychologically—has resigned... With regard to Sisters Scholastique and Marie-Bernard, it seems to us very important for the diocese to give its support to the legitimate superiors of the monastery. That even seems essential for their eventual re-integration into the community. The recent events give a negative impression in that they could be interpreted as a victory of the Sisters against their superiors.

The accusations against Sr. Gertrude were of particular concern.

We are very worried to note that Sr. Gertrude has been accused of taking part in the genocide. We would like you to give us your opinion; if this accusation is well-founded or if it is a calumny on the part of people who are opposed to her.

Refusing Marie-Bernard and Scholastique entry to the monastery was not merely intended to punish them. It was also meant to put the nuns who were still in Belgium on notice about the fate that awaited them, should they follow their example. Scholastique and Marie-Bernard spent the day at the monastery making communion wafers, but were obliged to return to the bishopric in the evening. For Marie-Bernard, the inability to live in their monastery marked an important step in the decision she took, a few months later, to leave the Church altogether.[45]

It drove us mad that we were not able to live in our own convent. I began to lose heart and I couldn't see any future for our monastery in Sovu or for our congregation. I could no longer see any Christianity in the community, with whites continuing to dictate what we could and could not do.

Having failed to expel Sr. Scholastique and Sr. Marie-Bernard from the order, the Church leaders made another attempt to convince them to withdraw their claims about what had taken place in Sovu during the genocide. The condition for their full re-integration into the monastery was elaborated in a letter, written by Fr. Nicolas Dayez on 7 March 1995 to Bishop Gahamanyi of Butare.

This gesture [of allowing them to spend the day at the monastery] on the part of the community of Sovu also calls for a gesture on the part of Sisters Scholastique and Marie-Bernard, with an aim of rebuilding the community on the basis of truth. They should at least recognise that they committed a serious offence and commit themselves to do everything to mitigate the consequences for the unity of the community. They must also, henceforth, abstain from spreading malicious talk which tarnishes the reputation of the community.
    [I]t must be made clear that in re-integrating into the monastery, the two Sisters, Scholastique and Marie-Bernard, remain under the unique authority of the Superior of Sovu. There is therefore no question of them receiving anyone at the monastery, of anyone living there except themselves. And even less a question of accepting someone who presents herself as wanting to be a part of the community (i.e. an applicant).

In August, Fr. André Comblin visited Rwanda with the specific purpose of "encouraging" Marie-Bernard and Scholastique to give written statements, absolving Sr. Gertrude and Sr. Kizito of any involvement in the genocide. Marie-Bernard gave the following account of his visit.

"Fr. Comblin himself came to harass us and to make us sign statements confirming the innocence of Gertrude and Kizito. We categorically refused to comply."

We told Comblin that he was not a magistrate and that he could not impose such conditions upon us. I asked him why they had not spoken out on behalf of the Tutsis during the genocide. He told me, to my face, that the Tutsis had to die. That outraged me even more, because he was trying to stop us thinking

---

[45] Sr. Marie-Bernard, who had taken her final vows on 22 April 1990, decided to leave the order on 28 December 1995. In March 1996, she received a response from the Vatican releasing her of all her vows.

about our loved ones who had died in the genocide. In the end, I wondered what had happened to the Gospel I had followed when I entered the community of nuns in 1984 and when I had taken my final vows in 1990.

In his report of the August visit, Fr. Comblin wrote of his meetings with Scholastique and Marie-Bernard.

The meetings took place in a hospitable climate, [characterised by] listening and by mutual respect. From my point of view, two questions had to be treated in a clear manner.

- the explicit recognition by the Sisters of the grave fault they committed when they left Belgium without the explicit permission of the Mother Superior who was then in charge.
   The two Sisters showed me the letter they sent to Fr. Nicholas, dated 18 March 1995. They consider this as acknowledging their fault.[46]
   They believe that the letter which Mother Marie-Jeanne sent them [dated 30 March 1995] shows that their excuses were accepted, and closes the chapter on this lapse and its consequences.

- the second point concerns the rumour, widespread in Belgium and in Rwanda, according to which the Mother [Superior] should be considered as a Rwandese *criminal*[47] who is hiding in Maredret. (*Solidaire* No.22 of 31 May 1995).
   But another rumour suggests that the Sisters who have returned to Rwanda are well-acquainted with these rumours.
   I put the question clearly to the Sisters who categorically deny having insinuated such things and to having spread such wicked statements.
   We are in agreement in saying that Sr. Gertrude had a formidable choice to make and that finally it was up to her to make the decision in good conscience. Perhaps she should have consulted with the Sisters? But the circumstances were so exceptional that it is impossible to say what was psychologically possible...

Saying that he wanted "to facilitate the road towards reconciliation," Fr. Comblin spelt out the necessary conditions.

- I am proposing to the Sisters that they should write and sign a paper where they make it known explicitly that they dissociate themselves from the rumours according to which Mother Gertrude is a criminal, with all the consequences that this implies.
   Sr. Scholastique said that she is in agreement with the content of the proposal but that she could not write it since I had not brought a written mandate. But that she would sign at the request of the Abbot or his replacement.
   Sr. Marie-Bernard believes that she could not sign anything without first having a dialogue with the community, either in Belgium or in Sovu.

- The Sisters are surprised by the efforts deployed to defend Sr. Gertrude while it seems that people want to forget the dead executed as a result of her decision to make the refugees leave because she wanted her community.
   One should not forget that Sr. Marie-Bernard lost two brothers that day... and without doubt it is not easy to distinguish between responsibility and guilt.
   Both the Sisters would like to have a dialogue with the community. They appreciate the offer of going to Belgium but unfortunately administrative difficulties seem to have prevented the meeting that we wanted.

Conclusion: We were able to approach the most delicate questions such as the situation in which the Sisters and Sr. Gertrude find themselves under these terrible circumstances.

---

[46] Their letter expresses regret "for the situation provoked by our return to Rwanda" but does not in fact acknowledge having committed a fault against Sr. Gertrude.
[47] Emphasis in the original text.

It seems to me that the next step should be the meeting of Sisters with the administrative Superior and of the representatives of the community, either in Belgium or in Sovu. The fact that they belong to the community of Sovu is not in question for the Sisters.

In the meantime, the Benedictines had been forced to deal with the publicity generated by the BBC documentary and the report from *African Rights*. In a signed press release, Abbot Cullen responded to a programme on the Belgian television station, RTBF, broadcast on 30 August.

> The accusations reported in this programme are based, according to their authors, on oral testimonies gathered in Belgium and elsewhere. Incidentally this is also the case with some of the written press. I can testify that what has been said consists of numerous errors. I am surprised that such serious suspicions could be raised about the two nuns [and that they] have been accused on the basis of such claims.
> I have myself been able to question people who were direct witnesses of the events which have been reported. What I have gathered about it formally contradicts the accusations which have been made.
> The truth is that Sr. Gertrude personally opened the monastery to welcome the refugees. With other Sisters, she took care to ensure that they were given food and treatment. She even helped some of them to escape. At the risk of her life, she did everything, not only for the refugees who were in her monastery, but also for the members of her community, by talking with the militiamen, by giving them money, by calling in the bourgmestre.

Without explaining the link, he added:

> Besides, it should not be forgotten that at the time of the subsequent evacuation of the community, nine Sisters were massacred.

To underline his belief in the innocence of the two nuns, Abbot Cullen wrote:

> I come from Ireland. I made this journey especially in order to reassure myself about everything that was being said and written about this matter. I am distressed to see such accusations levelled against nuns whose good faith and acts I cannot question.

In a subsequent joint letter, Abbot Cullen, the new Mother Superior of Sovu, Sr. Anastasie Mukamusoni and Fr. Nicolas Dayez wrote to Fr. Comblin to respond to his recommendations. Referring to the statement issued to the media, they wrote:

> This declaration has been triggered by the sudden publicity given in Belgium to this affair by the press and the television during the week which has just ended. The Sisters in general are accused and, in particular, Sr. Gertrude and Sr. Kizito are accused of having been "implicated in the genocide." When they cite the Sisters [making the accusations] in general, these reports don't exclude Sisters Scholastique and Marie-Bernard, but nor are they mentioned by name.
> Without any doubt, the simple fact of dissociating themselves would be, as you say, a help in order "to facilitate the road towards reconciliation." But this can only be a beginning. False accusations, we are convinced about it, have been made in Belgium and maybe also in Rwanda. Those which have been uttered in Belgium should be formally retracted, at a certain point, before the Sisters Scholastique and Marie-Bernard can be successfully re-integrated in their community.

It was not enough, they said, for Scholastique and Marie-Bernard to issue a statement absolving Sr. Gertrude and Sr. Kizito of involvement in the genocide.

> If the Sisters really are innocent, they should come to Belgium to prove their innocence. From our point of view, there is no other means of getting out of the current deadlock... The silence observed by Sisters Scholastique and Marie-Bernard at the end of a recent BBC documentary... which was defamatory for Sr. Gertrude and Sr. Kizito, was also surprising. In such a context, the silence in reality amounts to consent or an approval of what had been said in the documentary film in question.

They entrusted Fr. Comblin with a delicate task.

> We hope that you will persuade the two Sisters to take this important decision. Likewise [we hope that you will] convince them that we are not unaware of the sufferings that they endured, as well as the loss of their family in April-May 1994. But if this mitigates their responsibility, nevertheless it does not justify the accusations they have made against their Superior; and nor does it allow us to turn over a new leaf without speaking about it any more.

Immediately afterwards, steps were taken to bring Marie-Bernard and Scholastique to Belgium. A number of letters were written in July 1995 by Abbot Cullen and Fr. Dayez to the Belgian embassy in Kigali and to the immigration service in Rwanda to facilitate travel arrangements, but the visit did not materialise.

On 4 September, Abbot Cullen wrote to Fr. Comblin in preparation for his return to Rwanda. Scholastique's argument that she could not give Fr. Comblin a signed piece of paper absolving Gertrude of involvement in the genocide was uppermost in his mind.

> I had not thought of giving you a written mandate. I am attaching one now, since Sr. Scholastique seems to have demanded one before signing a retraction.
> The proposal you made to the Sisters is excellent: that they write and sign a paper where they make it clear that they are explicitly dissociating themselves from the rumours according to which Sr. Gertrude is a criminal with all the consequences that this entails. They should therefore distance themselves from the rumours which are going around about what happened in Sovu in April-May 1994, and should also confirm the innocence of Sr. Gertrude.

Fr. Comblin returned to Rwanda in October 1995. He was stopped at a roadblock, and his papers were confiscated and his visa was not renewed, forcing him to leave the country. With the charges against the Sisters of Sovu now widely known, Comblin's report and some other papers were printed by the local press.

On 14 February 1996, Fr. Jan Lenssen, the regional superior of the White Fathers, wrote to the then Minister of the Interior, Col. Alexis Kanyarengwe, to protest the treatment of Fr. Comblin, and publication of "a personal and confidential file of a spiritual content" in the local press. From his reaction, it is evident that Fr. Comblin's mission to convince Scholastique and Marie Bernard to remain silent about the genocide in Sovu was undertaken with the knowledge and blessing of his order. Lenssen characterised Fr. Comblin's mission as "personal and eminently pastoral."

> A personal and eminently pastoral initiative, aimed at helping to rebuild unity within a religious community, has proved harmful to my colleague, in his personal capacity, and to the spiritual mission which he had successfully undertaken for so long in the name of our Church, in order to build up "peace and unity" in our Church in Rwanda and in the country as a whole.

Fr. Lenssen expressed his regret at the refusal to prolong Fr. Comblin's visa.

> Fr. Comblin had requested an extension of his visa in order to continue his commitment to the Church which, in collaboration with the Conference of Bishops of the Rwandese Church, had duly appointed him to do so.
> Fr. Comblin has been a missionary here in Rwanda for a long time, working alongside its people in the search for peace and unity. His contribution to this work has proved more than satisfactory to everyone. The proof of this lies in the repeated requests by communities and people for a spiritual guide. His work is currently expanding and requests [for his services] are numerous. The programme which he would have to abandon in the case of a forced departure would suffer as there would be no one to take up his work.
> I do not wish make a fuss about the personal situation of this esteemed and ageing priest. However, I wonder how much harm this "legal measure" will do to his work and to him as an

individual. This attack will crush the spiritual vigour of a man totally dedicated to our Church and to the people of Rwanda.

The letter warned about the likely consequences.

It is clear that the process which your department has undertaken will have, Mr Minister, repercussions in the international press without the possibility of a representative of our organisation being able to inform them, with the best of intentions, beforehand. It is extremely regrettable that all of this could harm the efforts of the Church in Rwanda. It seems to me that the image and commitment of the country and its government would also be harmed.

This letter is intended to express my surprise, but most of all, to express the sorrow of the missionary family which, for a century, has shared the pain and the joy of the people of Rwanda through its Church, evangelisation and development work. We feel sorry that through the rejection of one of us, you may give the impression of rejecting the entirety of our work... [I] hope that the message I am sending you and the appeal that comes with it reaches you in a frame of mind which seeks to achieve understanding and collaboration with the work for peace and justice for our country and its people.

Fr. Comblin's faith in Sr. Gertrude has not wavered. In an interview with Belgian television in February 1999, he reiterated his belief in her innocence.

The journalist: Was the mission entrusted to you to bring back the two nuns who had fled? To bring them back to Belgium or was it rather to convince them that they should cease accusing Sr. Gertrude of participation in the genocide?

Fr. Comblin: Not at all, not at all. It was, firstly, to make them realise that they had been disobedient. And secondly, it was to see that they distanced themselves from the rumour which was going around, according to which Sr. Gertrude was a génocidaire.

The journalist: It was a rumour? Only?

Fr. Comblin: Ah! It was a rumour. That absolutely.

Asked if he was still believed Sr. Gertrude to be innocent, Fr. Comblin responded:

I am convinced about her innocence. It was a case of "we will kill the whole community, or you have to get rid of these people who have taken refuge in your place." I would say that she did what she had to.

The journalist, seeking further clarifications, pursued the question.

The journalist: That is to say that in some sense she sacrificed the refugees to save the community?

Fr. Comblin: But I think that at that moment, she had not sacrificed them. She dared to believe that she was going to save them.

The journalist: But nevertheless, not by sending them out?

Fr. Comblin: Yes, because she believed that the bourgmestre was on her side.

The journalist then read out an excerpt of the letter Sr. Gertrude wrote to the bourgmestre, on 5 May 1994, cited above, in which she asked "the administration of the commune to come and order all these people to return to their homes or to go elsewhere", adding "I am pleading with you Mr bourgmestre, to come and help us to settle this problem."[48]

---

48 "In the Name of the Law", RTBF television, February 1999.

Public Accusations

Despite all the efforts of the Benedictines, the accusations against Sr. Gertrude and Sr. Kizito were widely-publicised in Belgium in May 1995 after the newspaper of the Belgian Labour Party, *Solidaire*, published an article. On 26 August 1995, African Rights published a report, *Rwanda: Not So Innocent, When Women Become Killers*, which devoted a chapter to the accusations against Sr. Gertrude and Sr. Kizito. The story also caught the attention of the British media. In the words of one nun, "the curtain was lifted" on 25 August 1995, when BBC Television aired a 25-minute programme about the participation of women in the genocide. Part of the documentary was filmed in Sovu; many survivors spoke about their suffering at the hands of Sr. Gertrude and Sr. Kizito. Shortly afterwards, Kizito and some of the other nuns watched a video of the film together in Maredret; Gertrude was not there as she was living in Ermeton at the time. One of the nuns described Kizito's reaction.

> Kizito said that she didn't even know the people who were testifying against her.

Again, other members of the Catholic Church appeared unmoved by the accusations.

> Since the film was in English, there was a White Father who was translating into French for us. In his commentaries, he said that the film reflected lies.

The publicity which followed the publication of African Rights' report and the BBC documentary obliged the Benedictines to respond. But even in the face of the now consistent and chilling accounts of the nuns' involvement in the genocide, their position was only slightly shaken. Maintaining a dismissive attitude, some claimed that the allegations were without foundation, that they were the figment of the imagination of Tutsi nuns who are "traumatised." Others admitted that Sr. Gertrude forced the refugees to leave the monastery, but insist that she did so in order to save the lives of her Tutsi fellow-nuns.

In April 1997, Paul Ames of the Associated Press office in Brussels interviewed the head of the Benedictine order, Abbot Celestine Cullen who told him that "Those accusations were not well-founded."

> The Roman Catholic church describes the nuns as innocent refugees who fled the genocidal fury that swept their homeland in the spring of 1994 to find peace behind the high walls of Maredret. [T]he abbot acknowledged that Sister Gertrude had handed the Tutsis over to the Hutu militia. But she had done so only after threats to her nuns, and after assurances that the Tutsis would not be harmed, he said.[49]

Ames then went in search of the nuns. Struck, like other visitors to Maredret, by its physical beauty and tranquillity, he described the abbey as "a haven of religious solitude."

> Sisters Julienne and Gertrude, meanwhile, quietly go about their days at Maredret, where church leaders protect them even from the press. "The sisters have suffered enough. They are unjustly accused,' said Sister Bénédicte, the abbess at Maredret. 'I won't let you speak to them."[50]

On 4 September 1995, Albert van der Meulen, a Dutch journalist with RTL/Veronica TV visited Maredret, hoping to speak with Sr. Gertrude and Sr. Kizito. In a note to African Rights, he said that the Mother Superior told them "the Rwandese nuns were 'too emotional' to speak." He described the response when he confronted the Mother Superior with the findings in *Not So Innocent*.

---

[49] Paul Ames, AP despatch, 18 April 1997.
[50] *Ibid.*

They denied everything. They said you bought the witnesses, for £20 each. They said that Sister Julienne handed petrol to a truck-driver only to enable him to transport the wounded to the hospital. They said that in the convent they house 9 Hutu Sisters and 9 Tutsi Sisters and that there is no animosity among them whatsoever. That could not have been the case if two of them were killers. The Benedictine Sisters and Brothers of Maredsous have conducted an investigation, they say, and they have not found anyone from Butare who can or will confirm your allegations.

Philip Jacobson went to Maredret for an article he published in the London-based *Sunday Times Magazine* in January 1996. He described the response at the abbey when he asked to speak to the two nuns.

Knock at the great oak door to inquire about them, and a slight young nun will courteously but firmly decline to comment. It is a silence that speaks volumes.
 After the two Rwandan nuns were named and located, the only official comment from Maredsous was a terse, defensive statement. "We are convinced that these accusations are false," said Sister Françoise Janssens. "The correct attitude for us is silence."[51]

Despite the passage of time, there has been no shift in the attitude of the Benedictine order in Belgium. Belgian journalists who produced a programme for RTBF television in February 1999 visited the Benedictine monastery at Ermeton in an attempt to interview Sr. Gertrude and Sr. Kizito. A visibly agitated elderly European nun closed the door in their face, saying "they are not here."[52]

---

[51] "Blood Sisters", Philip Jacobson, *The Sunday Times Magazine*.
[52] "In the Name of the Law", RTBF.

Conclusion

Members of the Belgian Church have been anything but "silent" about the accusations against the Sisters of Sovu. They have been open in their support for Sr. Gertrude and Sr. Kizito, and in their criticisms of their accusers. By exerting undue pressure upon Sr. Scholastique, Sr. Marie-Bernard and the other nuns, they have sought to interfere with the process of justice. Their actions suggest that at the heart of the Catholic church in Belgium are clergy prepared not only to tolerate genocide suspects, but to work alongside them, and even to do all in their power to cover up for them. Some of them may have acted more out of blind faith in a colleague than out of any understanding of what happened in Sovu, but the consequence has been the same. Only a firm stand by the Belgian judicial authorities can make it clear that obstruction of justice is unacceptable. We believe that there are sufficient grounds for an inquiry.

The impunity that Sr. Gertrude and Sr. Kizito continue to enjoy is an immense source of pain to the survivors. Many of them have spoken of their wish that the nuns should face the charges against them in a court of law. With the strength of the evidence now available about the killings at Sovu, it is inconceivable that the nuns could continue to evade trial. Belgium has already opened a file on Sr. Gertrude, file number 62/95; but the case has dragged on, without any tangible results.

In the light of this case, it is important to make certain that Belgium is not now, and never again shall be, a haven for genocide suspects. A number of men accused of playing a prominent role in the genocide are living in Belgium. They include a man who occupied one of the most senior positions in the government that planned and implemented the genocide, Major-General Augustin Ndindiliyimana. He was chief of staff of the national gendarmerie, a force responsible for the deaths of hundreds of thousands of people. Others accused of playing a significant role include Vincent Ntezimana, an academic at the University of Butare, and Raymond Mugabo, a pupil in Butare who is now a university student. It is important to explore every possible avenue to advance the course of justice, either by bringing prosecutions in Belgium, or by handing suspects over to the ICTR. The background of the suspect, and the nature and level of political support they enjoy in Belgium, should not be a deterrent to investigations and prosecutions. Belgium has already co-operated with the ICTR. It sent investigators to Rwanda to examine the evidence against Joseph Kanyabashi, the bourgmestre of the town of Butare; he was subsequently extradited to the detention facilities of the ICTR in Arusha. It is necessary to show the same political resolve with respect to all the other cases—including the nuns of Sovu—to ensure that Belgium does not become a sanctuary for Rwandese génocidaires.